For Grade 2

Student Activity Workbook

Ready, Set, Show What You Know®

Activities to Build Skills for the Ohio Achievement Tests

Written By:
Andrea Karch Balas, Ph.D.
Judy Cafmeyer

Name:

Show What You Know®
Publishing

Published By:

Show What You Know® Publishing

A Division of Englefield & Associates, Inc.

P.O. Box 341348

Columbus, OH 43234-1348

614-764-1211

www.showwhatyouknowpublishing.com

Printed in the United States of America

07 06   20 19 18 17 16 15 14 13 12 11 10 9 8 7 6 5

ISBN: 1-59230-105-3

Limit of Liability/Disclaimer of Warranty: The authors and publishers have used their best efforts in preparing this book. Englefield & Associates, Inc., and the authors make no representation or warranties with respect to the contents of this book and specifically disclaim any implied warranties and shall in no event be liable for any loss of any kind including but not limited to special, incidental, consequential, or other damages.

About the Authors

Andrea Karch Balas, Ph.D., is an educator and a scientist who has taught both in the traditional classroom and in nonformal educational settings, from kindergarten to adult. Andrea has presented her research on the teaching and learning of science both nationally and internationally. Andrea received her doctorate in education from The Ohio State University and is currently the Science Coordinator in a private K–12 school. In addition to this book, Andrea is a co-author of the Ready, Set, Show What You Know® series for the Florida Comprehensive Assessment Tests (FCAT) for grades K–3 and the Ready, Set, Show What You Know® series for grades K–3 in Ohio.

Judy Cafmeyer has taught for 17 years in public and private schools from kindergarten to eighth grade. She is currently the supervisor for a Pre-K–8th grade instructional program. Judy also plans and presents teacher workshops related to Englefield and Associates, Inc., products. A graduate of The Ohio State University with a degree in elementary education, Judy has experienced education from various vantage points: as a teacher, as a representative on district curriculum committees, as a parent, as a volunteer, and as a school board officer. In addition to this book, Judy is a co-author of the Ready, Set, Show What You Know® series for the Florida Comprehensive Assessment Tests (FCAT) for grades K–3 and the Ready, Set, Show What You Know® series for grades K–3 in Ohio.

Acknowledgements

Show What You Know® Publishing acknowledges the following for their efforts in making this assessment preparation material available for Ohio students, parents, and teachers.

Cindi Englefield, President/Publisher
Eloise Boehm-Sasala, Vice President/Managing Editor
Lainie Burke, Project Editor/Graphic Designer
Erin Richers, Project Editor
Rob Ciccotelli, Project Editor
Christine Filippetti, Project Editor
Jill Borish, Project Editor
Jennifer Harney, Illustrator/Cover Designer

Content Reviewer:
Erica T. Klingerman

Table of Contents

Introduction

This workbook is designed to give you practice using skills that will help you prepare for the Ohio Achievement Tests.

It is very important that you read the directions carefully and do what the directions tell you to do. In this way, you will not only be preparing for the Ohio Achievement Tests, you will be practicing good test-taking habits.

There is a special certificate for you at the back of this book. When you have completed all of the pages in this workbook, write your name on the certificate and have your teacher or parent sign it too! This certificate congratulates you on your efforts and shows that you are becoming a proficient learner.

Writing

The Writing chapter of this workbook will help you continue building good writing habits. You will practice different skills that you are learning about in the writing process.

Good writing should always include:

- sentences that stay on topic,
- organized responses that have a beginning, a middle, and an end,
- a variety of words and sentences,
- the correct use of spelling, capitalization, and punctuation, and
- handwriting that is easily read by someone else.

Use this Writing Checklist to remind you to use good writing skills.

✔ Writing Checklist

☐ I read or listened to the directions carefully.

☐ I wrote complete sentences about the topic.

☐ I used a variety of words to make my writing interesting to read.

☐ I used different kinds of sentences in my writing.

☐ I checked my sentences for correct capitalization and punctuation.

☐ I used my best handwriting.

Directions: Look at the writing webs in the boxes below. Find the main idea for each web by looking at the supporting ideas around it. Fill in the main topic for each web on the line provided.

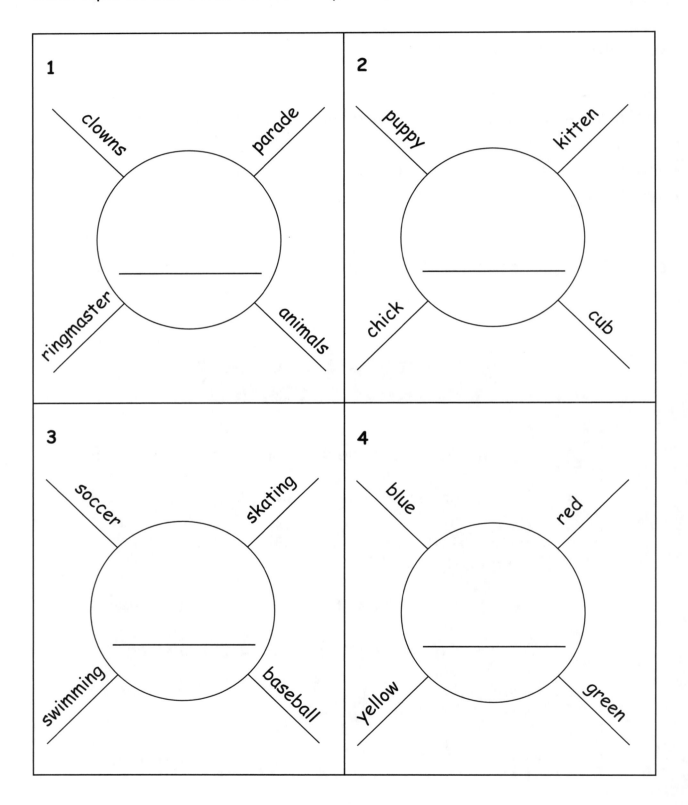

Directions: Read each writing selection below to decide who will be reading it (the audience). Next, decide why it was written (the purpose). Write your answers on the lines provided.

1.

Dear Aunt Mary,
    Thank you for the book. I really like it.
                    Love,
                    Jodi

Who is the audience?

_____

- - - - - - - - - - - - - - - - -

_____

What is the purpose for writing this piece?

- - - - - - - - - - - - - - - - -

2.

Lunch Menu
Grilled Cheese
Celery and Carrots
Peaches
Milk

Who is the audience?

_____

- - - - - - - - - - - - - - - - -

_____

What is the purpose for writing this piece?

_____

- - - - - - - - - - - - - - - - -

_____

3.

Homework:
- Spelling words
- Read story page 26
- Math problems 6-10

Who is the audience?

_____

- - - - - - - - - - - - - - - - -

_____

What is the purpose for writing this piece?

_____

- - - - - - - - - - - - - - - - -

Directions: Read each sentence carefully. Use a completely filled circle to show whether the sentence is declarative, interrogative, or exclamatory.

```
Declarative    —   statement

Exclamatory    —   emotion

Interrogative  —   question
```

	Declarative	Interrogative	Exclamatory
1. Who is buying lunch today?	◯	◯	◯
2. We went to the library last Saturday.	◯	◯	◯
3. Our team won the spelling contest.	◯	◯	◯
4. Look, it's snowing!	◯	◯	◯
5. What time is it, please?	◯	◯	◯
6. The parade starts at Main Street.	◯	◯	◯
7. My dog had five puppies!	◯	◯	◯

Directions: Read each sentence in the boxes below. Put the sentences in the correct order by numbering the boxes 1, 2, 3, 4, and 5. (Hint: Use the underlined linking words and phrases (transitions) to help you decide the correct order.)

<u>Finally</u>, Coach Larson thanks all of the parents for their help.

_____

<u>After the game</u>, both teams line up and shake hands.

_____

Coach Larson wants the team to learn how to be good sports.

1

_____

<u>At halftime</u>, the players on the other team are invited to share a fruit snack.

_____

<u>Before each game</u>, the team cheers for themselves and the other team.

_____

Directions: At the beginning of the year, Mrs. Carey made a bulletin board that looked like bank doors. Mrs. Carey told the students that they can deposit and withdraw words every day to improve their writing skills. The words are changed weekly to go with the topics the class is studying. The students named the bank after their teacher: Carey Word Bank.

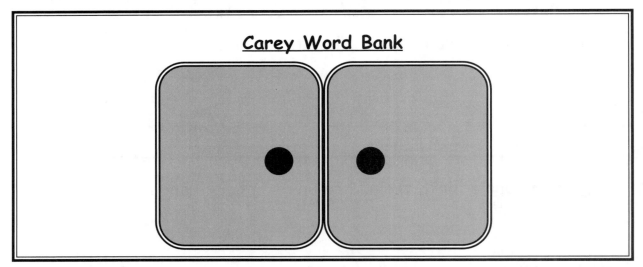

When the students open the doors of the word bank, a new list of words shows the topic for the week.

Carey Word Bank

dollar	gold	shiny	dime
cent	paper	bill	quarter
change	pennies	nickel	bank

1. Look at the words in the Carey Word Bank above to find the topic for the week. Write a complete sentence to show what topic the class is studying.

   _____

   _____

   _____

   _____

Directions: Withdraw or "select" a word from the Carey Word Bank to deposit or "complete" each of the following sentences. Words can be used more than once.

1. Henry put one ————————————— into his bank.

2. Five ———————————— equals one ———————————— .

3. That new quarter is ———————————— !

4. Did you get ————————————— from your dollar?

5. The boy has a ————————————— chain.

6. William traded two dimes and a nickel for a ———————————— .

7. The teacher collected ———————————— for the field trip.

Directions: Use your proofreading skills to help you correct the capitalization, punctuation, and spelling mistakes in the paragraph below.

Enrique and his brother are going

to the <u>toledo</u> Zoo on <u>saturday</u> __
        (1)   (2)   (3)

<u>they</u> want <u>two</u> see <u>ther</u> favorite
 (4)   (5)   (6)

<u>animls</u>. <u>uncl</u> <u>carlos</u> <u>iz</u> meeting
 (7)   (8)   (9) (10)

them at the front gate__
                 (11)

1. _____
2. _____
3. _____
4. _____
5. _____
6. _____
7. _____
8. _____
9. _____
10. _____
11. _____

Directions: Use your best handwriting to rewrite the following paragraph. Be sure to correct the spelling of the underlined words.

Anita <u>road</u> her <u>bice</u> to the <u>stor</u>. Her mother <u>wantd</u> <u>sum</u> <u>bred</u> and milk. She <u>gav</u> her a five dollar <u>Bill</u>. <u>Dos</u> Anita <u>hav</u> enough money to <u>by</u> <u>bothe</u> items?

Directions: Mr. Dials put the following information on the chalkboard to help the students write an invitation for someone to attend the art show at Fairfield Elementary School. Use the information shown on the chalkboard to invite someone to the art show. Be sure your invitation includes the date, a greeting, a body, a closing, and your signature.

Fairfield Elementary Art Show

Wednesday, March 2

7:00 p.m.

Directions: Draw a line to match the writing piece in the left column to the reason it was written (purpose) in the right column.

1.

| Monday, February 7th |
| The high school band came to our school. I liked the tuba the best! |

writing a poem

2.

| Mom, |
| Mrs. Clark called. Please call her back. |
| Beth |

writing a note

3.

| Music lesson at 4 p.m. |
| Soccer practice on Friday. |
| Bake sale Saturday. |

writing a message

4.

| My kite flew high, |
| Into the sky. |
| And I saw, |
| A bird go by. |

writing a journal

Directions: Write a poem, note, message, or journal entry on the lines below. Use the models on page 11 to help you. Use your best handwriting.

Directions: Use a completely filled circle to select the correctly spelled word in each box. Then, use your best handwriting to write that word on the line.

year ⭕	yer ⭕	

doz ⭕	does ⭕	

smal ⭕	small ⭕	

leave ⭕	leve ⭕	

rase ⭕	race ⭕	

coat ⭕	koat ⭕	

Directions: Look at each picture. Write the consonant blend on the line that completes the correct word.

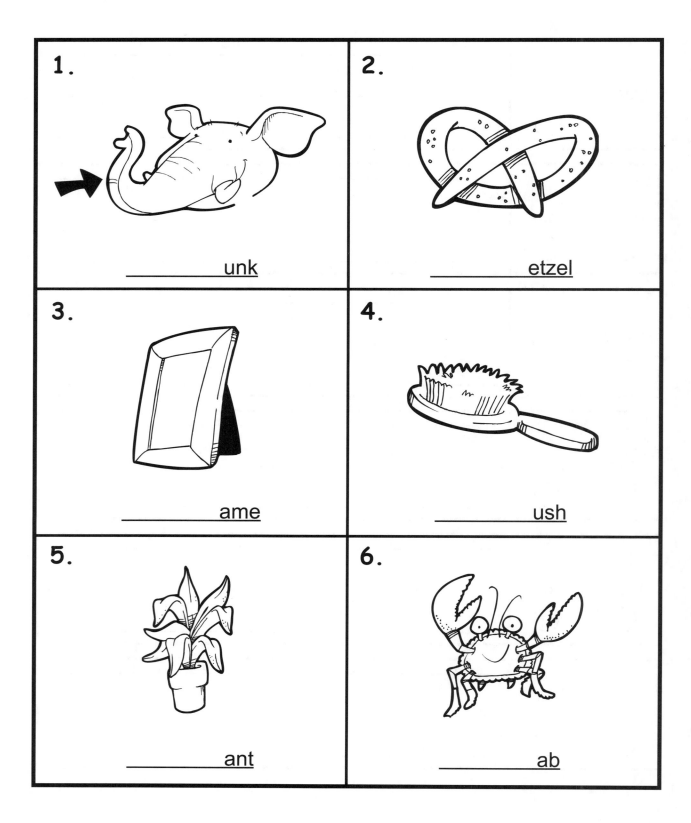

1.

_____ unk

2.

_____ etzel

3.

_____ ame

4.

_____ ush

5.

_____ ant

6.

_____ ab

Directions: Make each of the nouns below plural by adding *-s* or *-es* to the end of the word. Write the new word on the line.

1. chair

2. dish

3. clock

4. glove

5. rabbit

6. shovel

7. box

8. class

Directions: Look at each of the contractions below. Use a completely filled circle to select the contraction that has the apostrophe (') in the correct place. The first one has been done for you.

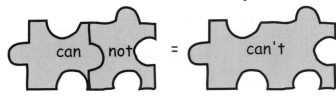

1.   Ia'm   I'm   Iam'
     ○   ●   ○

2.   didn't   did'nt   didno't
     ○   ○   ○

3.   iti's   it's   i'ts
     ○   ○   ○

4.   youw'll   you'wll   you'll
     ○   ○   ○

5.   hav'nt   haven't   havno't
     ○   ○   ○

6.   I've   Ihav'e   Ih've
     ○   ○   ○

Directions: Rewrite the invitation below using your best handwriting. Be sure to correct all of the capitalization and punctuation mistakes.

may 22 2005

dear principal jones

you are invited to our second-grade class picnic.

the picnic will be held at sunnyside elementary school on june 12 2005

sincerely

dani

Directions: Read each sentence carefully. Look at the underlined word and decide if it is a noun (person, place, or thing), a verb (an action word), or an adjective (a describing word).

	Noun	Verb	Adjective
1. I <u>live</u> in Ohio.	◯	◯	◯
2. The children are <u>happy</u>.	◯	◯	◯
3. Some <u>people</u> like to fish.	◯	◯	◯
4. <u>Oak</u> trees are strong.	◯	◯	◯
5. Will <u>stepped</u> outside.	◯	◯	◯
6. <u>Sheila</u> sang a song.	◯	◯	◯
7. Does the <u>puppy</u> like you?	◯	◯	◯

Directions: Rewrite each sentence below using a personal pronoun for the underlined word or phrase. The first one has been done for you.

Personal Pronouns
he, she, it, his, her, we, us, our, they

---

1. Color <u>the apple</u> red.

   Color it red.

2. <u>Billy</u> runs fast.

3. Where are <u>the girls</u>?

4. <u>Mike and I</u> went to the movie.

5. Today is <u>Sara's</u> birthday.

6. <u>March</u> is a windy month.

Directions: Read each of the sentences carefully. Use a completely filled circle to show the correct verb tense. The first one has been done for you.

	Past Tense	Present Tense	Future Tense
1. Joey walked his dog.	●	○	○
2. Cody likes to play soccer.	○	○	○
3. She went to the library.	○	○	○
4. Ebony will come later.	○	○	○
5. The clock struck twelve.	○	○	○
6. The picnic is today!	○	○	○
7. Will you be there tomorrow?	○	○	○
8. Jill invited me to her party.	○	○	○
9. The flowers died.	○	○	○
10. I fed the fish this morning.	○	○	○

Directions: Look at the words in the box. Sort the words into three different groups (categories). Then write the words on the lines provided.

cow	daisy	hat	dandelion
rose	shirt	chicken	coat
shoes	pig	violet	sheep

Group #1	Group #2	Group #3
animals	flowers	clothing

Directions: Choose one group of words from page 21 and write three sentences using these words. (Reminder: Use proper capitalization, punctuation, and your best handwriting.)

Directions: Mr. Bell wants his second graders to learn good speaking skills when presenting reports to the class. He wrote some rules on the board that the students must always follow. Mr. Bell's rules are shown in the box below. Read the rules carefully, then decide whether his students are following them. Use a completely filled circle to answer yes or no.

Mr. Bell's Rules for Good Speaking

1. Always look at your audience when you're speaking to them.
2. Always speak clearly and loud enough to be heard by your audience.
3. Always present your ideas in order with a beginning, a middle, and an end.

	Yes	No
1. Becky shouted her information to the audience.	○	○
2. Will looked up at the ceiling as he talked.	○	○
3. Mary Beth used notecards to keep her speech in order.	○	○
4. Matt looked at the class when he gave his report.	○	○
5. The class could not hear Carly when she talked.	○	○

The Reading chapter of this workbook will help you use information from different types of written resources:

- stories,
- poems,
- charts,
- tables, and
- graphs.

You are asked to read, refer to, and answer questions about fiction and nonfiction passages by using a completely filled circle for multiple-choice answers, writing a word, a phrase, or a sentence for a short answer, or writing several sentences and giving more details to explain your answers for an extended response.

Use this Reading Checklist to help you understand the reading passages and complete the workbook pages in this chapter.

✔ Reading Checklist

☐ I read or listened to the directions that were given.

☐ I read or listened to the reading passages carefully.

☐ I used context clues to help me understand the reading selection.

☐ I can identify different types of literature selections.

☐ I answered all the questions on the page.

Directions: Match each word in the first column to its rhyming word partner in the second column. Then, write another rhyming word on the line in the third column. The first one has been done for you.

1. base   rain

plane

2. cane   same

3. axe   lace

4. deer   tacks

5. aim   light

6. write   fear

7. soap   clay

8. day   rope

Directions: Read the list of sight words in the box. Then, answer the questions that follow.

find	basketball	dinner
wasn't	his	look
swish	Mr.	yellow
Friday	night	suddenly

1. Write the words that have short ĭ sounds.

_____ _____ _____

_____ _____ _____

_____ _____ _____

2. Write the word that is an abbreviation.

_____

_____

3. Write the words that have one syllable.

_____

_____

_____

_____

Directions: Use a completely filled circle to mark each item that begins with the same beginning blend sound as the word "truck."

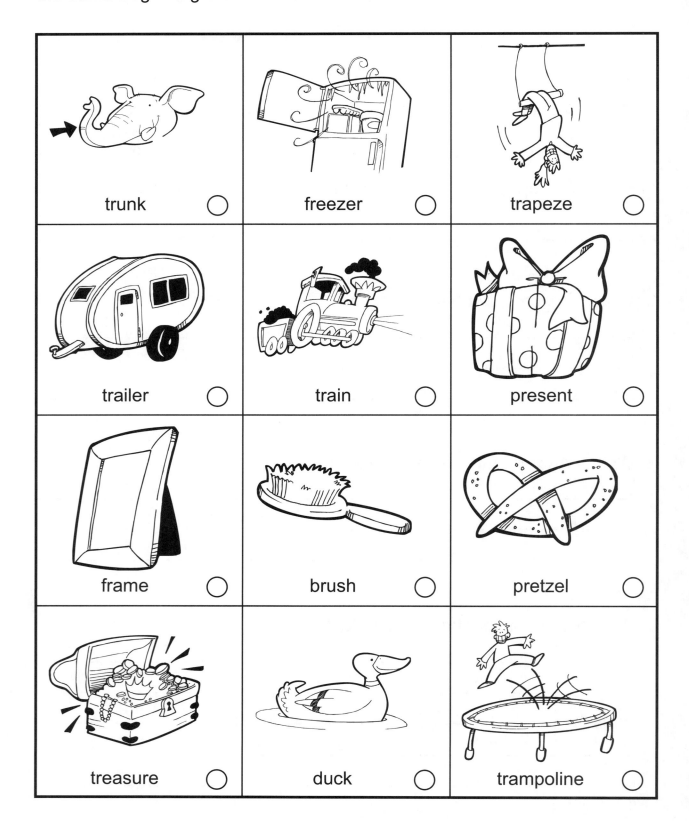

trunk ○	freezer ○	trapeze ○
trailer ○	train ○	present ○
frame ○	brush ○	pretzel ○
treasure ○	duck ○	trampoline ○

Directions: For each picture, find the letter that shows the ending sound of the word. Use a completely filled circle to mark your answer choice.

1. crab

○ b
○ s
○ t

2. button

○ b
○ n
○ s

3. door

○ g
○ b
○ r

4. glass

○ n
○ s
○ g

5. mitten

○ n
○ t
○ m

6. bird

○ b
○ r
○ d

7. ladybug

○ g
○ l
○ d

8. plant

○ c
○ p
○ t

Directions: Read each of the sentences carefully. Listen for words that have more than one syllable in them. Underline the multi-syllable words you find in each sentence, then write the number of multi-syllable words you found in the box provided. The first one had been done for you.

> **Definition:** Words are divided into parts called syllables. Every syllable has a vowel sound.
>
> yellow = yel low = 2 syllables

1. The <u>children</u> were <u>happy</u> to use gold <u>glitter</u> on their art <u>projects</u>.

   4

2. The Clark family went to the airport on Monday.

3. Megan saw a herd of buffalo at the national park she was visiting.

4. Grandpa saw the rabbits eating the carrots in his garden.

5. Thanksgiving is always the fourth Thursday in November.

Directions: Read each of the sentences carefully. Look at the underlined word and decide whether the vowel has a long sound or a short sound in it. Use a completely filled circle to mark your answer choice.

	Long Vowel	Short Vowel
1. Lee was a <u>king</u> in the school play.	◯	◯
2. Please hang your <u>coat</u> in the closet.	◯	◯
3. <u>Hold</u> this basket of vegetables.	◯	◯
4. <u>We</u> are going to the lake on Sunday.	◯	◯
5. The <u>wind</u> blew the kite high into the sky.	◯	◯
6. The clock read half <u>past</u> two.	◯	◯

Directions: Use the sentences on page 31 to complete this page.

1. Find two words that are not underlined that have long vowel sounds. Write them below.

   _____   _____

   _____   _____

2. Find two words that are not underlined that have short vowel sounds. Write them below.

   _____   _____

   _____   _____

3. Find two words that can be read with a long vowel sound or a short vowel sound. Write them below.

   _____   _____

   _____   _____

4. Write a new sentence using one of the underlined words.

   _____

   _____

   _____

   _____

Directions: Synonyms are words that have **similar** meanings. Read each sentence carefully. Then, use a completely filled circle to show the synonym for the underlined word.

1. The <u>cup</u> is full.

   ◯ glass   ◯ bowl   ◯ mug

2. Put the <u>bag</u> on the table.

   ◯ box   ◯ sack   ◯ basket

3. The thunder made a loud <u>noise</u>.

   ◯ sound   ◯ spark   ◯ speaker

4. Maria <u>chose</u> the pink flowers.

   ◯ gave   ◯ sent   ◯ picked

5. José put the sand in the <u>bucket</u>.

   ◯ pail   ◯ basket   ◯ tub

6. I <u>sent</u> my aunt a letter.

   ◯ gave   ◯ mailed   ◯ wrote

7. The cat fell asleep on the <u>rug</u>.

   ◯ floor   ◯ carpet   ◯ step

8. Keep your desks <u>tidy</u>.

   ◯ neat   ◯ together   ◯ straight

Directions: Antonyms are words that have **opposite** meanings. Match the word in the left column to its antonym in the right column. The first one has been done for you.

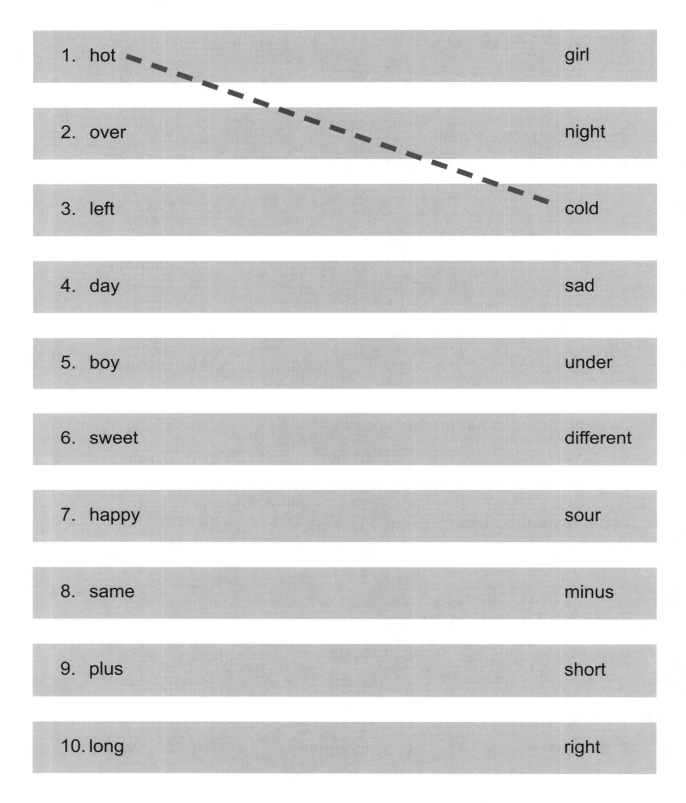

1. hot   girl

2. over   night

3. left   cold

4. day   sad

5. boy   under

6. sweet   different

7. happy   sour

8. same   minus

9. plus   short

10. long   right

Directions: Match each word in the left column with a word in the right column to form a compound word. The first one has been done for you. Trace over the dashed line to practice matching the two words.

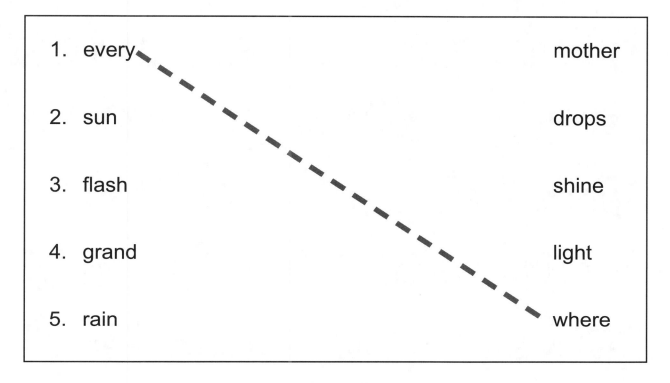

1. every   mother

2. sun   drops

3. flash   shine

4. grand   light

5. rain   where

Directions: Write the compound word under each picture. Tell how the two words in each compound word are related.

6.

7.

Directions: Match the word in the left column to its correct abbreviation in the right column. The first one has been done for you.

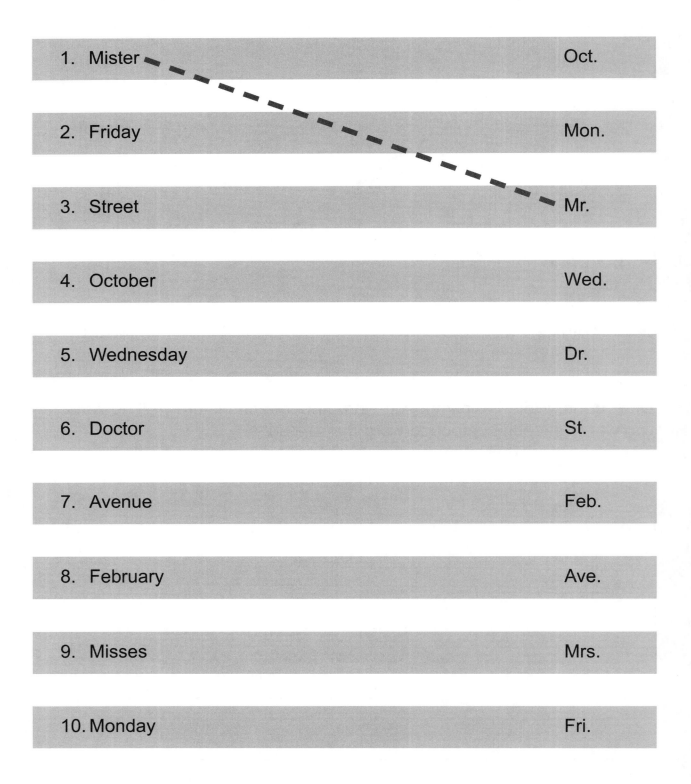

1. Mister   Oct.

2. Friday   Mon.

3. Street   Mr.

4. October   Wed.

5. Wednesday   Dr.

6. Doctor   St.

7. Avenue   Feb.

8. February   Ave.

9. Misses   Mrs.

10. Monday   Fri.

Directions: Draw a line to match the two words in the left column to the correct contraction in the right column.

1. have not	I'm
2. you will	haven't
3. I am	wouldn't
4. it is	you'll
5. would not	don't
6. cannot	it's
7. do not	won't
8. we will	can't
9. will not	let's
10. let us	we'll

Directions: Rewrite the following sentences using a contraction for the underlined word.

1. Emily <u>could not</u> take Mrs. Brown's dog for a walk today.

2. <u>We will</u> bring the sandwiches to Mr. Daley's picnic.

3. We <u>do not</u> have school on Monday, Sept. 20th.

Directions: Combine the prefix and the root word to form a new word. Write the new word on the line. Then, answer the question that follows.

A **prefix** is a syllable at the beginning of a word.

	Prefix	+	Root Word	=	New Word
1.	un	+	happy	=	
2.	re	+	write	=	
3.	un	+	able	=	
4.	pre	+	pay	=	
5.	re	+	turn	=	

Read the two sentences below carefully.

1. I must <u>write</u> my name neatly.

2. I must <u>rewrite</u> my name neatly.

Explain how the prefix in sentence 2 changed the context (meaning) of the sentence.

_____

_____

_____

_____

_____

Directions: Combine the root word and the suffix to form a new word. Write the new word on the line. Then, answer the questions that follows.

A **suffix** is a syllable added to the end of a word.

Root Word	+	Suffix	=	New Word
1. farm	+	er	=	_____
2. use	+	ful	=	_____
3. fast	+	est	=	_____
4. home	+	less	=	_____
5. long	+	er	=	_____

Read the two sentences below carefully.

1. Harry's dog has a <u>long</u> tail.
2. Harry's dog has a <u>longer</u> tail.

Write a new sentence using the word *long* and the *-est* suffix.

_____

_____

Explain how the context (meaning) of the sentence changes when you add this suffix.

_____

_____

Directions: Randy had to record all of the different reasons he used for reading from the time he awoke until he got to school. Read the following information from Randy's journal to determine whether he was reading to be informed, to follow directions, or to be entertained. Use a completely filled circle to mark your answer choice.

	To Be Informed	To Follow Directions	To Be Entertained
1. Randy read his favorite comic strip in the newspaper.	○	○	○
2. Randy opened a new box of breakfast cereal using the instructions on the box top.	○	○	○
3. Randy read the safety signs at the bus stop.	○	○	○
4. Randy went through the door marked "Entrance" at the school building.	○	○	○
5. Randy picked a magazine with an article about bats to use to write his report.	○	○	○

Directions: Read the story below. Use the information from the story and the information you already know about bicycles and tricycles to help you fill in the Venn diagram on page 43. A Venn diagram helps you compare two items. Use the Venn diagram to find other ways the two toys are the same or different.

Sidney and Matt's Big Surprise

Sidney and Matt were jumping with excitement waiting for Grandpa to arrive. When the children talked to Grandpa on Sunday, he told them he had a big surprise for each of them. Just then, the doorbell rang. The two children ran to the door, expecting to greet their Grandpa. Two large boxes were sitting on the doorstep. Both boxes had big bows on them. The one with a purple bow had Sidney's name on it. The one with a red bow had Matt's name on it. "Surprise!" came a voice from behind the two boxes. It was Grandpa!

Sidney and Matt opened the boxes. One child found a new blue bicycle, and the other child saw a new red tricycle. Both children hugged Grandpa and thanked him for the big surprises.

Sidney and Matt stared at their new toys sparkling in the sunshine. The two children compared the two toys by noticing how they were alike and how they were different.

Here are some of the things that Sidney and Matt noticed about their toys.

- Both of the toys are new.
- The bicycle is bigger than the tricycle.
- Both of them have wheels.
- The tricycle has three wheels, and the bicycle has two wheels.

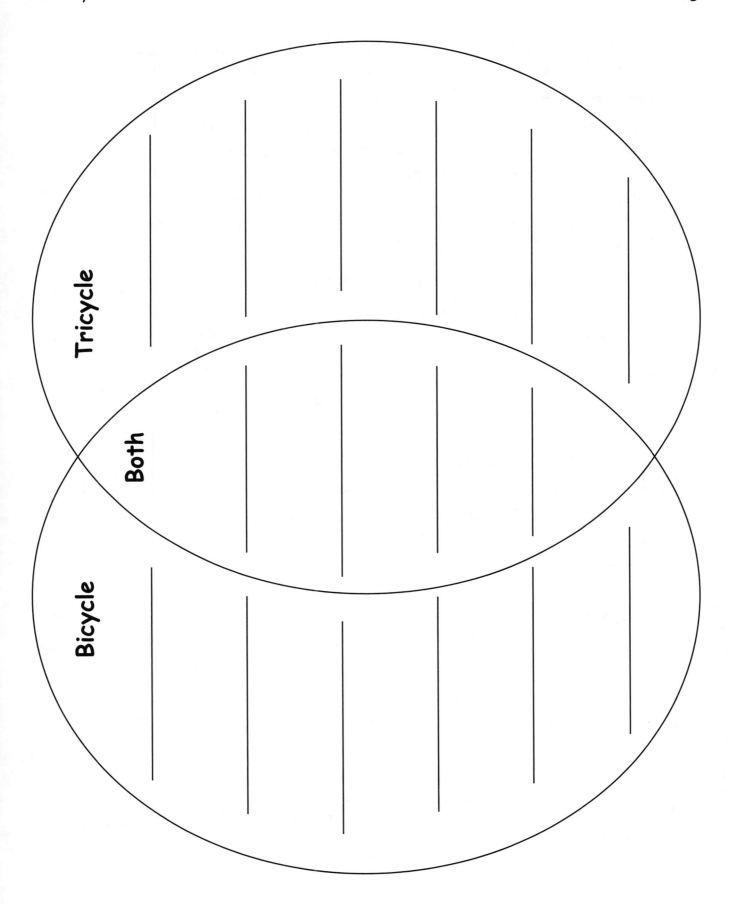

Directions: Read the passage below. Then, answer the four questions about it. Write a few words or a complete sentence to answer each item.

Mr. Greene's second-grade class is reading and learning about the environment. The class wants to help the environment by saving natural resources. The students want others to do the same. They decide to start a classroom project to reuse and recycle things people use every day. The following list shows five things the class wants everyone to do.

1. Write on both sides of their papers.
2. Put extra paper in a box to use for art projects.
3. Collect aluminum cans to recycle.
4. Use lunch boxes or reuse lunch bags.
5. Make signs that tell others why recycling is important.

1. Whose class is learning about the environment?

    _____

    _—_

    _____

2. What is the message of this passage?

    _____

    _—_

    _____

3. What is one activity the class is trying to get others to do?

    _____

    _—_

    _____

4. After reading the passage, how do you feel about recycling to save natural resources?

    _____

    _—_

    _____

Directions: Ms. Balas created this poster for the classroom library to remind students why they might choose certain reading materials.

Enjoyment—personal choice reading material

Literary Experience—choosing from a variety of reading materials, such as novels, storybooks, poetry, etc.

Gain Information—choose specific selections to learn facts and details about a special subject

Perform a Task—choose specific materials to learn how to complete a special activity

1. Tony wants to teach his dog some new tricks.

　○ enjoyment 　　　○ literary experience 　　　○ perform a task

2. Tyler likes to read various kinds of literature.

　○ literary experience 　　　○ gain information 　　　○ perform a task

3. Marci reads mystery books by her favorite author.

　○ enjoyment 　　　○ literary experience 　　　○ gain information

4. Keith wonders why snakes shed their skin.

　○ enjoyment 　　　○ gain information 　　　○ perform a task

Directions: Read the information and definitions below. Use them to help you label the diagram on the next page.

1. The giraffe is the tallest animal that lives on land. It can grow to be 19 feet tall. The giraffe's height helps it to find food at the top of trees. The giraffe eats leaves, twigs, and bark from the trees.

2. A giraffe's coat is made up of different sized brown patches on a tan background. The brown shapes are larger on the giraffe's body, with smaller brown shapes on its face and legs. The giraffe can hide among the trees because its body covering acts as camouflage for it. Giraffes have two small horns. The male giraffe has knobbed, hairless horns and the female has thinner, tufted horns.

3. The natural environment for giraffes is the savanna or grassland in Africa. Giraffes also live in zoos in the United States and around the world.

Glossary

camouflage coat:	patches of different sizes and colors that help giraffes hide
fringed tail:	helps the giraffe to swat flies and pests
horns:	males have hairless, knobbed horns; females have thinner, tufted horns
long neck:	can reach into tall trees
long tongue:	helps the giraffe strip leaves off trees
mane:	the long, tough hairs on the neck of a giraffe

Directions: Use the information from page 46 to label the diagram below.

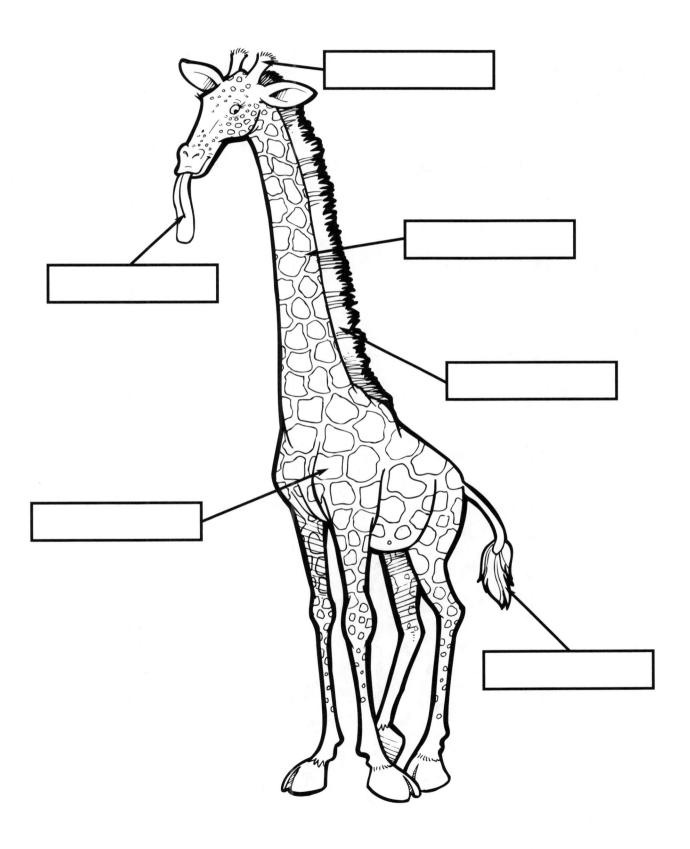

Identify Information (2 of 2)

Directions: Use what you know about the giraffe to answer the following questions. Use a completely filled circle to mark your answer choice.

1. <u>What</u> food does the giraffe eat?

   ○ meat   ○ fish   ○ leaves

2. <u>Where</u> are the smaller brown patches found on the giraffe's body?

   ○ face   ○ body   ○ neck

3. <u>How</u> tall can a giraffe be?

   ○ 91 feet   ○ 19 inches   ○ 19 feet

4. <u>Who</u> is the tallest land animal?

   ○ bear   ○ giraffe   ○ ostrich

5. <u>How</u> does the giraffe's coat protect it?

   ○ It is a   ○ It scares   ○ It's pretty.
     camouflage   other animals.

6. <u>Why</u> can the giraffe get food from tall trees?

   ○ fringed tail   ○ horns   ○ long neck

Directions: Reread the paragraphs about giraffes on page 46 to help you fill in the boxes on this page.

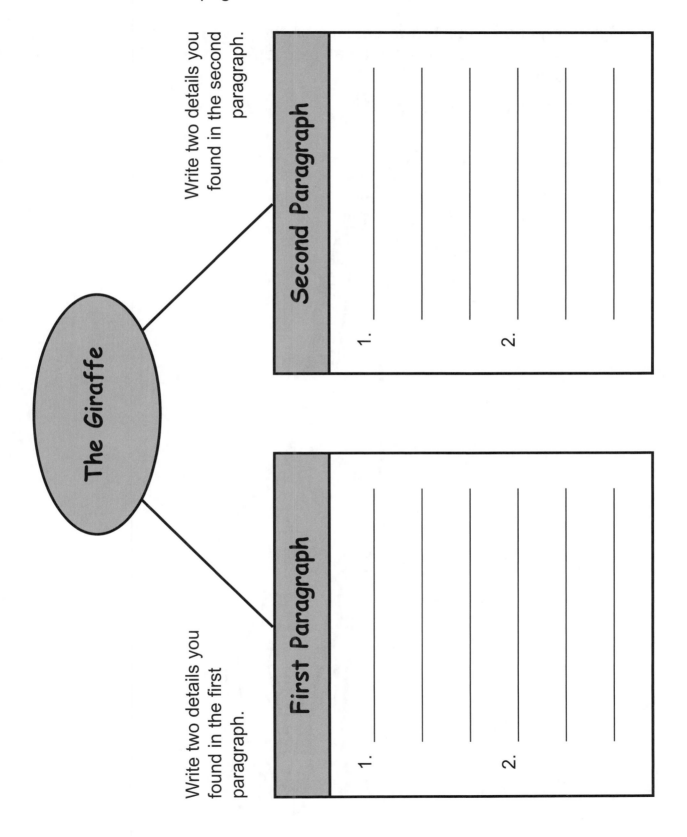

Write two details you found in the second paragraph.

Second Paragraph

1.

2.

The Giraffe

Write two details you found in the first paragraph.

First Paragraph

1.

2.

Directions: Complete the giraffe illustration by following these instructions.

1. Draw a tall tree next to the giraffe.

2. Color large and small brown patches on the giraffe's body. Where are the large patches? Where are the small patches? (Hint: Use the information on page 46.)

3. Draw a fringed tail on the giraffe.

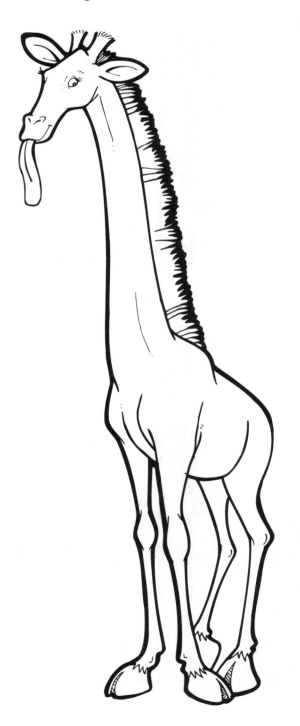

Directions: Read the story below. Use the Venn diagram on the next page to compare a traditional version of the Three Little Pigs to the version in this book.

Three Little Pigs
by Judy Cafmeyer

Once upon a time, there were three little pigs. They liked to grow vegetables.

The first little pig liked to grow carrots. The second little pig liked to grow green beans. And the third little pig liked to grow tomatoes.

One day, the three pigs decided to take their vegetables to the market and sell them. The first little pig put his carrots in a basket and away he went. The second little pig put his green beans in a basket and away he went. The third little pig put his tomatoes in a basket and away he went.

Each of the little pigs was skipping happily along his path to the market, when suddenly, all three pigs collided. Colors of orange, green, and red speckled the sky. Carrots, green beans, and tomatoes flew everywhere!

The first little pig shouted, "My carrots are ruined!"

The second little pig yelled, "My green beans are ruined!"

The third little pig screamed, "My tomatoes are ruined!"

The three pigs were sitting on the side of the road crying about their bad luck when a big, bad wolf arrived. The wolf saw the mixed-up vegetables and suggested that the mess could be useful. The vegetables could be used for a soup, and the soup could be sold at the market. And so, together, the four of them made soup.

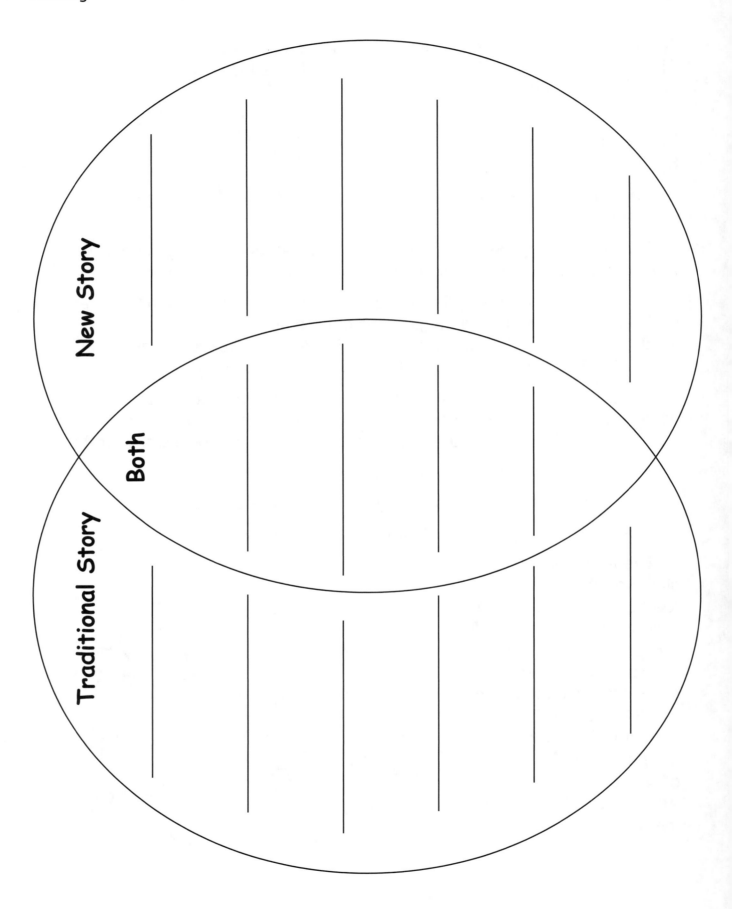

New Story

Both

Traditional Story

Directions: Refer to the story on page 51 to help you answer the questions about it. Use a completely filled circle to mark your answer choice.

1. Which little pig grew green beans?

    first little pig   second little pig   third little pig
        ◯   ◯   ◯

2. Which vegetable is NOT grown by the little pigs?

    carrots   beets   beans
        ◯   ◯   ◯

3. In this version of the Three Little Pigs, the main characters

    built houses.   grew vegetables.   raised chickens.
        ◯   ◯   ◯

4. What is the setting of this story?

    a vegetable garden   the woods   a path to the market
        ◯   ◯   ◯

5. Describe the big, bad wolf in this version of the Three Little Pigs.

    _____

    _____

    _____

    _____

    _____

    _____

Characters and Setting   53

Directions: Some words can appeal to our five senses—taste, touch, see, smell, and hear. Read the word (or words) in the left column and decide what sense it suggests. Use a completely filled circle to mark your answer choice.

1. **sticky**

    taste ○   smell ○   touch ○

2. **sweet**

    touch ○   taste ○   hear ○

3. **crunchy**

    smell ○   hear ○   see ○

4. **crispy**

    smell ○   hear ○   see ○

5. **the howling wind**

    hear ○   see ○   touch ○

6. **soft and velvety**

    taste ○   see ○   touch ○

7. **sour**

    taste ○   see ○   touch ○

8. **golden sunset**

    see ○   hear ○   smell ○

9. **stinky socks**

    smell ○   touch ○   see ○

Mathematics

In the Mathematics chapter of this workbook, you will be practicing different types of problem-solving skills. Some of the worksheets ask you to read a short paragraph and answer some questions about it. At times, you will need to look at illustrations, graphs, or tables to find the information to complete the questions you are asked. You might be asked to show how you got your answer by solving the math problems inside a boxed area or an open space.

Use a completely filled circle to respond to multiple-choice questions, and write a word, a phrase, or a complete a sentence for short-answers.

Use this Mathematics Checklist to help you carefully complete your workbook pages.

☑ **Mathematics Checklist**

☐ I read or listened to the problem information carefully.

☐ I read or listened to the directions carefully and understood what I was supposed to do.

☐ I followed the directions that were given.

☐ I completed all the problems on the page.

☐ I checked my work.

Directions: Put the numbers into the correct place value column. The first one has been done for you.

	thousands	hundreds	tens	ones
a. 500	0	5	0	0
b. 27				
c. 303				
d. 90				
e. 100				
f. 4,000				
g. 907				
h. 40				
i. 901				
j. 6,500				

Directions: Look at the 3-digit number in each box. It can be written in different ways. The first one has been done for you.

461

four hundred sixty-one

__4__ hundreds

__6__ tens   __46__ tens

__1__ ones   __1__ ones

__4__ hundreds & __61__ ones

804

_____

_____ hundreds

_____ tens   _____ tens

_____ ones   _____ ones

_____ hundreds & _____ ones

753

_____

_____ hundreds

_____ tens   _____ tens

_____ ones   _____ ones

_____ hundreds & _____ ones

229

_____

_____ hundreds

_____ tens   _____ tens

_____ ones   _____ ones

_____ hundreds & _____ ones

Directions: On the line provided, write the correct number for each number name.

1. four hundred sixty-one   _____

2. twenty-five   _____

3. six thousand two hundred forty-eight   _____

4. three hundred thirty-three   _____

5. seventy-six   _____

6. five hundred twenty   _____

7. two thousand sixteen   _____

8. forty-nine   _____

9. one hundred ninety-nine   _____

10. eighty-seven   _____

Directions: Joey is learning to count money and make change from one dollar. Look at the item in the left column. Write the cost of the item on the line in the middle column. Subtract the cost from $1.00. Draw the coins that show the correct change in the last column. The first one has been done for you.

1. $0.40 $0.40	$1.00 − .40 —————— .60	25¢ 25¢ 10¢
2. $0.95 $0.95	$1.00 − —————— .	
3. $0.50 $0.50	$1.00 − —————— .	
4. $0.75 $0.75	$1.00 − —————— .	
5. $0.85 $0.85	$1.00 − —————— .	
6. $0.25 $0.25	$1.00 − —————— .	

Directions: Mrs. Smith gave Kayla, George, and Rena some money to buy gifts at the toy store. Use the extra space below each story problem to show your work as you solve it. Use a completely filled circle to answer "Yes" or "No" to each question.

Kayla	George	Rena
$1.85	$2.25	$1.55

Toy Store Gifts

bubbles	$0.50
ball	$0.10
yo-yo	$1.00
toy car	$0.20
jump rope	$0.70
balloon	$0.45

                                                    Yes   No

1. Kayla wants to buy bubbles, a ball, a yo-yo, and a toy car. Does she have enough money to buy all four items?   ◯   ◯

2. George wants to buy all six items listed on the toy store gifts list. Does he have enough money?   ◯   ◯

3. Rena wants to buy a yo-yo and two balls. Does she have enough money?   ◯   ◯

Directions: Answer the four questions based on prices of the items pictured. Show your work in the extra space.

1. Mr. Garrett bought one gear and one spring. How much did he spend?

   $_____ . _____

2. Mr. Garrett needs a new wrench and a new screwdriver. How much will it cost him to buy both of these items?

   $_____ . _____

3. Mr. Garrett has $5.00. If he buys one gear, one spring, one wrench, and one screwdriver, does he have any money left?

   ◯ Yes   ◯ No

4. Mr. Garrett has $5.00. If he buys one gear, one spring, one wrench, and one screwdriver, does he have enough money to buy a toolbox?

   ◯ Yes   ◯ No

Directions: Identify the fraction that matches the shaded area in the shape pictured. Use a completely filled circle to mark your answer choice.

1.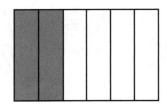

○ $\frac{1}{6}$

○ $\frac{4}{6}$

○ $\frac{2}{6}$

2.

○ $\frac{1}{8}$

○ $\frac{4}{8}$

○ $\frac{7}{8}$

3.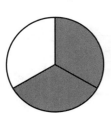

○ $\frac{1}{3}$

○ $\frac{2}{3}$

○ $\frac{3}{3}$

4.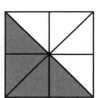

○ $\frac{1}{8}$

○ $\frac{3}{8}$

○ $\frac{4}{8}$

5.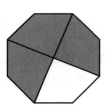

○ $\frac{1}{4}$

○ $\frac{3}{4}$

○ $\frac{2}{4}$

6.

○ $\frac{1}{4}$

○ $\frac{3}{4}$

○ $\frac{1}{2}$

Directions: Match each fraction name in the left column to the correct commonly-used fraction in the right column. The first one has been done for you.

1. one-half	$\dfrac{1}{4}$
2. one-third	$\dfrac{2}{3}$
3. one-fourth	$\dfrac{5}{6}$
4. one-fifth	$\dfrac{3}{4}$
5. one-sixth	$\dfrac{1}{2}$
6. two-thirds	$\dfrac{1}{6}$
7. three-fourths	$\dfrac{1}{3}$
8. five-sixths	$\dfrac{1}{5}$

Directions: Read each of the following word problems. Then, in the box provided, write an addition or subtraction number sentence (equation) to solve each problem. Use the extra space to help you work the problems.

1. Tamara counted 8 red birds, 7 yellow birds, and 13 black birds sitting on a wire in her backyard. How many birds did she count?

$$8$$
$$7$$
$$+\ 13$$
———————

——————— **birds**

2. If 22 yellow birds are in the tree, and 18 yellow birds fly away, how many yellow birds will there be?

3. If there are 48 birds sitting on a wire and 27 birds fly away, how many birds are left?

4. Tamara counted a total of 65 birds sitting on a wire in her backyard. If 13 birds are there now, how many have flown away?

Directions: Match the addition problem in the left column to the multiplication problem it equals in the right column. (Hint: How many times is the same number repeated in the addition problem?) The first one has been done for you.

a. 2 + 2 + 2 + 2 + 2 + 2 + 2 + 2 + 2   8 x 2

b. 5 + 5 + 5 + 5 + 5   1 x 7

c. 8 + 8   3 x 6

d. 1 + 1 + 1 + 1 + 1 + 1 + 1   10 x 4

e. 4 + 4 + 4 + 4 + 4 + 4 + 4 + 4   2 x 9

f. 10 + 10 + 10 + 10   5 x 5

g. 3 + 3 + 3 + 3 + 3 + 3   9 x 5

h. 7 + 7 + 7 + 7 + 7 + 7   4 x 8

i. 6 + 6 + 6 + 6 + 6 + 6 + 6 + 6 + 6 + 6   7 x 6

j. 9 + 9 + 9 + 9 + 9   6 x 10

Represent Multiplication as Repeated Addition

Directions: Cut out the apple slices on page 67 to answer the four questions below. Division is repeated subtraction: (12 – 3) – 3) – 3) – 3). Count the apple slices and write an equation that shows how the apple slices can be shared equally using the repeated subtraction method.

1. If four children share these apple slices equally, how many apple slices will each child receive?

2. If six children share these apple slices equally, how many apple slices will each child receive?

3. If two children share these apple slices equally, how many apple slices will each child receive?

4. If three children share these apple slices equally, how many apple slices will each child receive?

5. If no one shares the apple slices with you, how many apple slices will you have?

Directions: Cut out each apple slice along the outside edge. Use the apple slices to answer the questions on page 66.

Directions: Count the number of jelly beans in each hand. Read the directions in each box to add or subtract 10 beans. Use a completely filled circle to mark your answer choice.

1. Add 10	2. Subtract 10

1. **Add 10**

10   20   30
○   ○   ○

2. **Subtract 10**

10   20   30
○   ○   ○

3. **Subtract 10**

5   15   25
○   ○   ○

4. **Add 10**

2   12   22
○   ○   ○

5. **Add 10**

16   26   36
○   ○   ○

6. **Subtract 10**

15   25   35
○   ○   ○

Directions: Use front-end estimation to find the estimated cost for each item. Use a completely filled circle to mark your answer choice.

1. $5.89
   - ○ $5.00
   - ○ $0.90

2. $4.50
   - ○ $5.00
   - ○ $4.00

3. CHOCOLATE $0.50
   - ○ $1.00
   - ○ $0.50

4. $0.59
   - ○ $0.50
   - ○ $0.60

5. $10.50
   - ○ $11.00
   - ○ $10.00

6. $1.39
   - ○ $0.39
   - ○ $1.00

7. $3.99
   - ○ $4.00
   - ○ $3.00

8. $1.29
   - ○ $1.00
   - ○ $1.29

9. $6.50
   - ○ $0.50
   - ○ $6.00

10. $0.25
    - ○ $0.30
    - ○ $0.20

11. $9.99
    - ○ $9.00
    - ○ $8.00

12. $4.85
    - ○ $4.00
    - ○ $5.00

Directions: Read the sentences in the left column. Decide what is being measured: time, length, weight, or volume. Use a completely filled circle to mark your answer choice. The first one has been done for you.

	time	length	weight	volume
1. John's bookshelf is 48 cm high.	○	●	○	○
2. The lunch bell rings at 11:45 a.m.	○	○	○	○
3. Marie is 38 inches tall.	○	○	○	○
4. I want to know how much my dog weighs.	○	○	○	○
5. There are 2 minutes left in the football game.	○	○	○	○
6. Dad bought 3 gallons of milk at the store.	○	○	○	○
7. Morning recess begins at 10:00 a.m.	○	○	○	○
8. Gary is 20 pounds heavier than his dog.	○	○	○	○
9. Mother bought 2 yards of fabric at the store.	○	○	○	○
10. The oatmeal was in the microwave for 60 seconds.	○	○	○	○

Select Appropriate Units of Measure

Directions: Mrs. Smith used the chart below to help the students understand how to measure using metric units.

length
one centimeter = the width of a finger

volume
two liters = a large bottle of soda pop

weight
one gram = a small paper clip

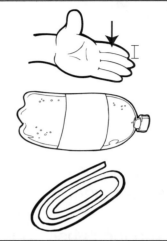

1. Ruby is making punch for the party. She needs two large bottles of soda pop. How many liters will she use?

   _____

2. The paper airplane weighs as much as 16 small paper clips. How much does the airplane weigh?

   _____

3. About how many centimeters is the width of this page?

   _____

   How did you get your measurement?

   _____

   _____

Directions: Read each story problem. Look at the two clocks and choose the clock that answers the question. Use a completely filled circle to mark your answer choice.

1. James had to be home by 3:00 p.m. He was five minutes early. What time did James get home?

    ○    ○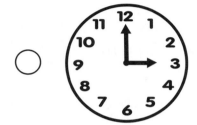

2. Evonne goes to bed at 8:30 p.m. She gets up at 7:30 a.m. Which clock shows what time Evonne goes to bed?

    ○    ○

3. Jamey gets on the school bus at 8:00 a.m. She arrives at school 15 minutes later. What time does Jamey arrive at school?

    ○ 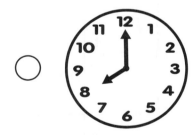   ○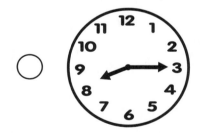

4. The second grade goes to lunch at noon. Recess begins at 12:15 p.m. Which clock shows when lunch begins?

    ○ 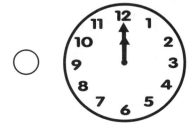   ○

Tell Time to the Nearest 5 Minute Interval

Directions: Read the information below. Use a completely filled circle to show the time that correctly answers each question. Use the boxes on the right to show your work.

1. The baseball game started at 1:20 p.m. The game lasted two hours. What time did the game end?

   ○ 3:15 p.m.   ○ 3:20 p.m.   ○ 3:25 p.m.

2. Teresa leaves for school at 8:37 a.m. She gets up one hour before she leaves. What time does Teresa get up in the morning?

   ○ 7:35 a.m.   ○ 7:36 a.m.   ○ 7:37 a.m.

3. Gerald is going to the park after school. It takes 15 minutes to get to the park. School lets out at 3:18 p.m. What time will Gerald arrive at the park?

   ○ 3:15 p.m.   ○ 3:18 p.m.   ○ 3:33 p.m.

4. Mara went to the beach at 11:05 a.m. She stayed there for one and a half hours. What time did she leave the beach?

   ○ 11:35 a.m.   ○ 12:05 p.m.   ○ 12:35 p.m.

Directions: Cut out the ruler at the bottom of the page along the dotted lines. Use the ruler to measure the items on page 77 in inches (in) and in centimeters (cm).

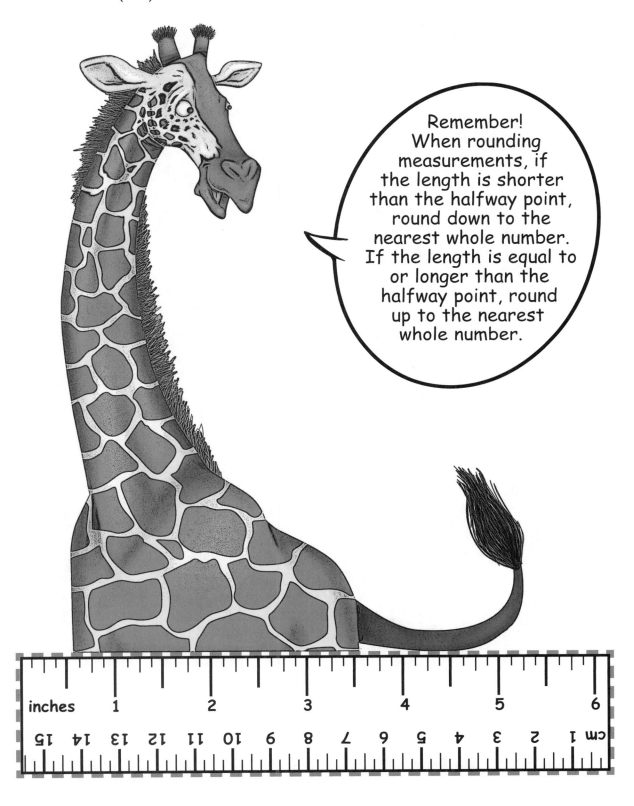

Remember! When rounding measurements, if the length is shorter than the halfway point, round down to the nearest whole number. If the length is equal to or longer than the halfway point, round up to the nearest whole number.

inches   1   2   3   4   5   6

cm 1   2   3   4   5   6   7   8   9   10   11   12   13   14   15

Directions: Use the ruler from page 75 to measure each item in inches (in) and in centimeters (cm). Round each measurement to the nearest whole number. Write the length of each item in the correct column.

	inches	centimeters
1.	_____	_____
2.	_____	_____
3.	_____	_____
4.	_____	_____
5.	_____	_____
6.	_____	_____

Directions: Read each sentence to decide which measuring tool is needed for each activity. Cut out the measuring tools on page 79. Glue the correct tool in the box next to the activity it goes with.

1. Deshawn wants to know the outside temperature.	
2. Tina is measuring flour for a cookie recipe.	
3. Raymond is checking the amount of rainfall after a storm.	
4. Lee is measuring the growth of his bean plants.	
5. Ricardo is counting the days until his birthday.	
6. Alysha's grandmother is arriving on the early bus.	

Directions: Cut out the measuring tools below along the dotted lines. Glue each tool next to the sentence that describes one of its uses in the activity on page 78.

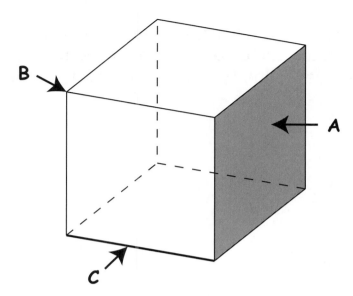

Directions: Look at the 3-dimensional cube above. Then, answer the questions about the diagram. Use a completely filled circle to mark your answer choice.

	A	B	C
1. A vertex is a point where two straight lines meet. A corner is a vertex. Which letter points to a vertex?	○	○	○
2. Which letter points to a face, or surface, of the cube?	○	○	○
3. Two sides meet at the edge of a 3-dimensional figure. Which letter points to an edge?	○	○	○

4. Color the face of the cone red. Draw an arrow to show the vertex of the cone.

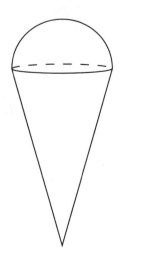

Directions: Compare the two figures in the left column. If the two figures are the same shape and the same size, they are congruent. Use a completely filled circle to mark "yes" if the figures are congruent or "no" if they are not congruent.

		Yes	No
1.	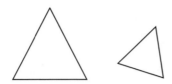	◯	◯
2.		◯	◯
3.		◯	◯
4.		◯	◯
5.		◯	◯
6.		◯	◯
7.		◯	◯
8.		◯	◯

Directions: Draw a line of symmetry through each figure in the left column. In the right column, draw a line to divide the figure into non-symmetrical parts. The first one has been done for you.

Symmetrical	Non-symmetrical

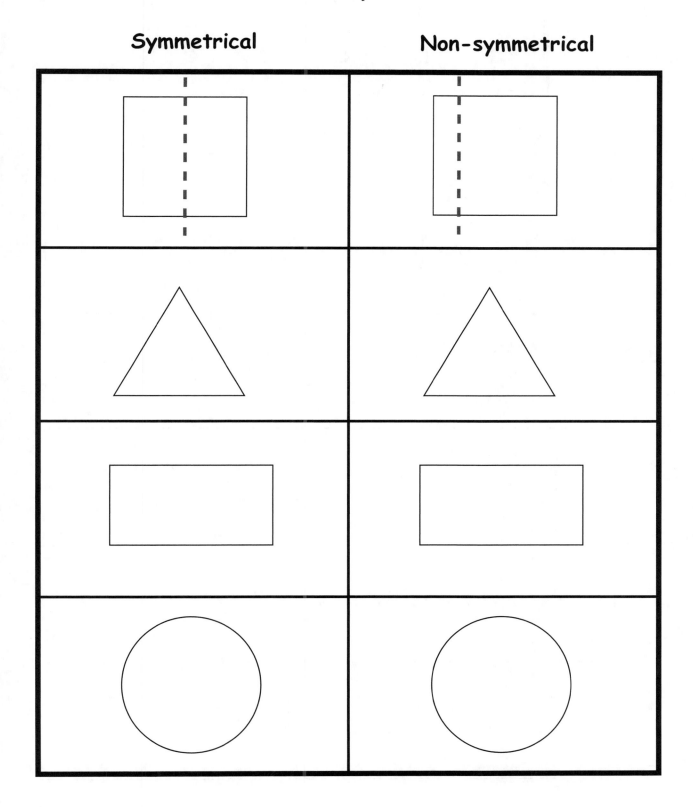

Directions: Use the correct letters from the key to complete each pattern.

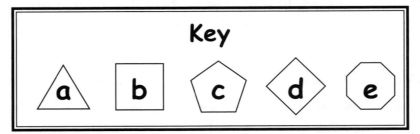

Key

a   b   c   d   e

1.

a a c c

2.

3.

4.

5.

6.

Directions: Use a completely filled circle to select the answer choice that correctly completes each sequence.

1. _____   **lunch**   **dinner**
   ◯ snack   ◯ breakfast   ◯ supper

2. **34**   **35**   _____
   ◯ 37   ◯ 33   ◯ 36

3. **1:00**   **2:00**   _____
   ◯ 3:00   ◯ 5:00   ◯ 12:00

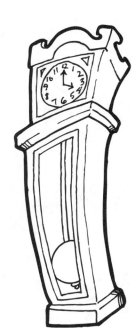

4. **tenth**   **eleventh**   _____
   ◯ fourth   ◯ twelfth   ◯ ninth

5. _____   **Sunday**   **Monday**
   ◯ Saturday   ◯ Friday   ◯ Tuesday

6. **March**   _____   **May**
   ◯ June   ◯ February   ◯ April

Determine Missing Elements

Directions: Write the number on the line that correctly completes each sequence. Draw a line to match each sequence to its rule. The first one has been done for you.

a. 5, __10__, 15, 20   The rule is to subtract 10.

b. _____, 17, 14, 11   The rule is to add 4.

c. 150, _____, 152, 153   The rule is to add 2.

d. 32, 34, _____, 38   The rule is to add 5.

e. 25, 28, 31, _____   The rule is to subtract 5.

f. 60, _____, 40, 30   The rule is to add 3.

g. 4, 8, _____, 16   The rule is to add 1.

h. 45, 40, 35, _____   The rule is to subtract 3.

Directions: A number is missing in each of the addition problems below. A ☐ is used to show that a number is missing. Find the missing number for each problem. Use a completely filled circle to mark your answer choice. The first one has been done for you.

1. 16 + ☐ = 18   ● 2   ○ 3   ○ 4

2. 25 + 21 = ☐   ○ 44   ○ 46   ○ 64

3. ☐ + 11 = 74   ○ 36   ○ 58   ○ 63

4. 18 + ☐ = 48   ○ 20   ○ 30   ○ 40

5. 12 + 44 = ☐   ○ 36   ○ 46   ○ 56

6. ☐ + 10 = 95   ○ 15   ○ 75   ○ 85

7. 58 + ☐ = 79   ○ 21   ○ 12   ○ 32

8. 101 + 26 = ☐   ○ 109   ○ 126   ○ 127

Identify Values for Symbols in an Equation   87

Directions: A number is missing in each of the subtraction problems below. A is used to show that a number is missing. Find the missing number for each problem. Use a completely filled circle to mark your answer choice. The first one has been done for you.

1. 49 − ☐ = 30   ○ 20   ● 19   ○ 79

2. ☐ − 23 = 36   ○ 55   ○ 59   ○ 86

3. 44 − 11 = ☐   ○ 23   ○ 33   ○ 43

4. 88 − ☐ = 44   ○ 35   ○ 41   ○ 44

5. ☐ − 12 = 52   ○ 66   ○ 64   ○ 46

6. 95 − 10 = ☐   ○ 15   ○ 75   ○ 85

7. 58 − ☐ = 37   ○ 21   ○ 12   ○ 32

8. 117 − 16 = ☐   ○ 109   ○ 101   ○ 121

Directions: Read each sentence. Use a completely filled circle to show whether each sentence describes qualitative or quantitative changes.

> **Qualitative:** describes how something changes
>
> **Quantitative:** tells how much something changes using numbers

	Qualitative	Quantitative
1. Tim grew 2 inches this year.	○	○
2. Tina arrived later than Robert.	○	○
3. The dog ate more biscuits today.	○	○
4. The temperature dropped 10 degrees this morning.	○	○
5. The lake is 2 miles wider than the river	○	○
6. The team won the race by several seconds.	○	○
7. Jack is shorter than the tall bean stalk.	○	○
8. It rained one and one-half inches less this month than last month.	○	○

Directions: Megan asked each student in her class to name his or her favorite sport. She recorded the results on a picture graph. Use the data (information) from her picture graph to answer the questions below.

Students' Favorite Sports

soccer	⚽ ⚽ ⚽ ⚽ ⚽ ⚽
basketball	🏀 🏀 🏀 🏀 🏀 🏀 🏀 🏀 🏀
baseball	⚾ ⚾ ⚾ ⚾
tennis	🎾 🎾 🎾 🎾 🎾 🎾 🎾

* Each ball equals one vote.

1. How many students participated in Megan's
   data collection?   _____

2. How many more votes did tennis get
   than soccer?   _____

3. How many students like basketball best?   _____

4. How many students like baseball best?   _____

5. Subtract the smallest number of votes on
   the graph from the largest number of votes on
   the graph to find the **range** of Megan's data.   _____

Directions: Cut out the dates and glue them on the timeline in correct chronological order.

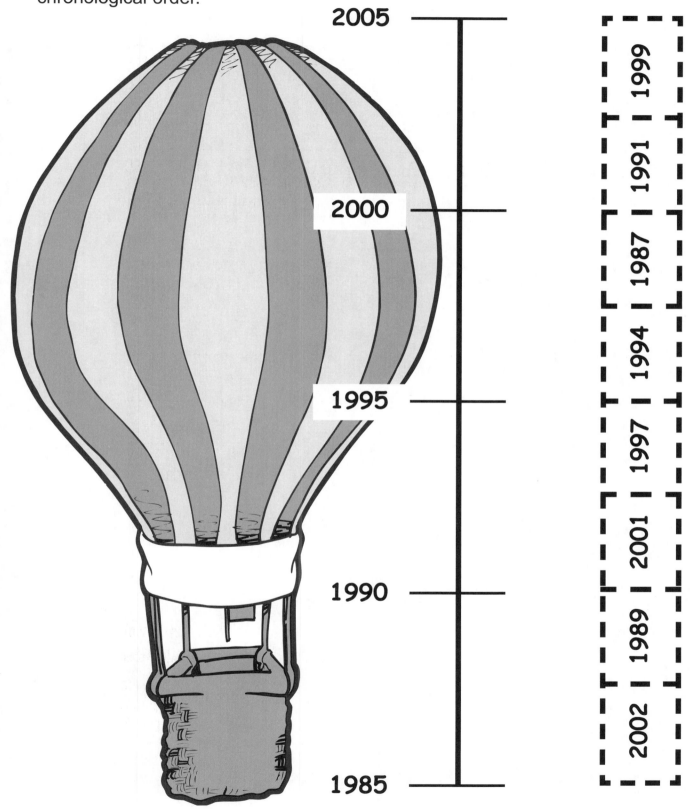

2005

2000

1995

1990

1985

1999

1991

1987

1994

1997

2001

1989

2002

Directions: Look at the **picture graph** and the **bar graph** below. Answer the questions to compare the data. Use a completely filled circle to mark your answer choice.

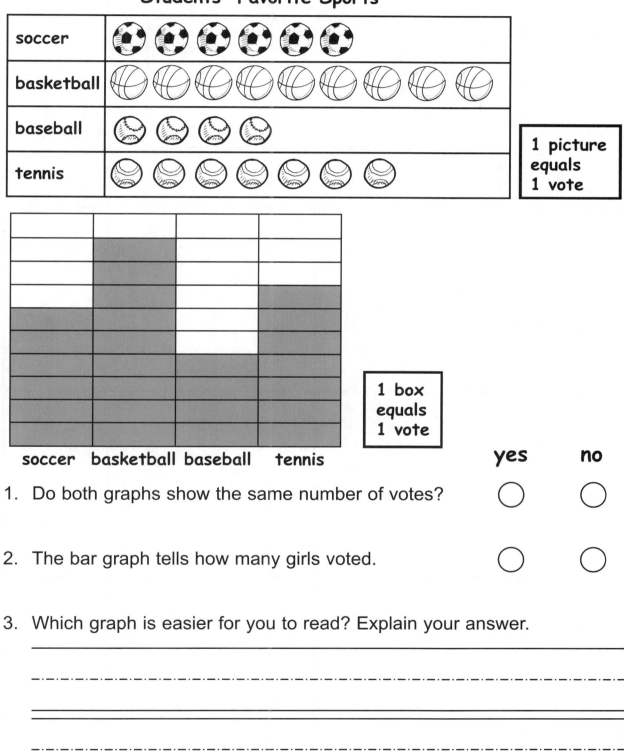

Students' Favorite Sports

1 picture equals 1 vote

1 box equals 1 vote

soccer basketball baseball tennis

                                                    yes   **no**

1. Do both graphs show the same number of votes?   ◯   ◯

2. The bar graph tells how many girls voted.   ◯   ◯

3. Which graph is easier for you to read? Explain your answer.

_____

_____

_____

_____

Directions: Look at the three shapes in the box below. Draw five different combinations using these shapes in the boxes. One combination has been done for you.

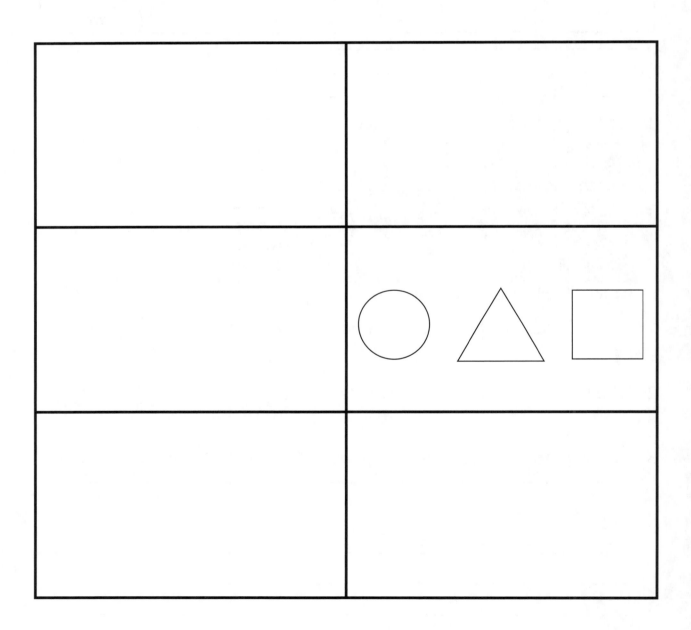

Use Pictures to Represent Possible Arrangements

Directions: Rearrange the numerals in the box below to make six different number combinations.

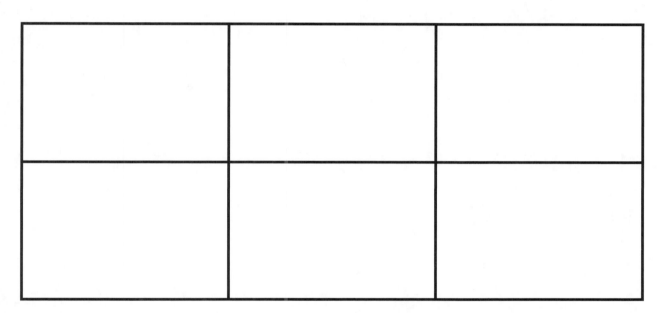

1. What is the largest number you can make using these numerals? _____

2. What is the smallest number you can make? _____

3. Write all of the numbers you can make that have a 6 in the tens position using the numerals 4, 5, and 6.

_____

_____

Social Studies

The activities in this chapter of this workbook will help you practice your Social Studies skills. You will be asked to use different types of information to answer the questions. There will be some short reading passages with questions for you to answer about the information you read. You will be asked to use tables, maps, and illustrations to answer some questions.

You will be answering three different kinds of questions. A completely filled circle will be used for multiple-choice answers. Write a word, a phrase, or a complete sentence for a short-answer, and write more sentences with details for an extended-response.

Use this Social Studies Checklist to help you check your answers on the workbook pages.

✔ Social Studies Checklist

☐ I read or listened to the information given on the page.

☐ I followed directions that were given.

☐ I used the tables, maps, or graphs to help me understand and answer the questions.

☐ I filled in circles or wrote complete answers to the questions I was asked.

☐ I answered all the questions on the page.

☐ I checked my answers carefully.

Directions: Complete the calendar below by filling in the missing numbers. Then, answer the questions about it.

Sunday	Monday	Tuesday	Wednesday	Thursday	Friday	Saturday
		1				5
			9			
13				17		
	21				25	
		29				

1. How many days are in a week? _____

2. How many days are there in the month shown on this calendar? _____

3. On what day does this month begin? _____

4. On what day does this month end? _____

5. What day is the 7th of the month? _____

6. A picnic is planned for the 24th day of the month. What day of the week is it? _____

Directions: Look at the birthday timeline below. It is divided into boxes that show the months of the year. Read the four sentences that follow. Write the name of the student in the correct box on the timeline.

Birthday Timeline

Jan., Feb., March	April, May, June	July, Aug., Sept.	Oct., Nov., Dec.

1. Maggie celebrated her birthday on the last day of school in June.

2. Alex was born on February 29th.

3. Ellie has her birthday on the Fourth of July.

4. Corrie was born on the last day of the year.

Place Events in Chronological Order

Directions: Read the selection below, then follow the directions on the next page.

Patrick likes going to his grandparents' house. When he is there, he likes to look at the photo albums that his grandma keeps on the bookshelves. Patrick usually looks at the albums that have pictures of his family. He likes to see how he and his brother Sam and his sister Emma change as they get older. Patrick's grandma takes lots of pictures because Sam, Emma, and Patrick are growing up so quickly.

One day, Patrick decided to look at the photo album that was on the bottom shelf. As he was looking at the pictures, he saw some people that looked like his family. But Patrick did not know these people. He went to ask his grandma about the pictures.

Patrick picked out a picture that showed a woman hanging laundry on a clothesline. The woman looked like his own mother. Patrick's grandmother told him that the picture was of her mother, Patrick's great-grandmother. She explained that her mother would hang clothes outside to dry instead of using the electric dryer when the weather was nice.

Patrick paged through the album and found a picture of his grandfather shoveling snow when he was about Patrick's age. The snow looked really deep, and his grandfather was using a shovel. Patrick remembered watching his grandfather clean snow off the driveway last winter, but he used a snowblower. That machine made the job go easier and faster.

Patrick put the photo album back on the bottom shelf. He knew he would pick that album the next time he went to his grandparents' house.

Directions: Use the information in the reading selection on page 100 to draw the photographs Patrick saw in the album.

Patrick's great-grandmother is hanging laundry.

Patrick's grandfather is shoveling snow.

Directions: The second-grade teacher took a class survey to find out from which continents the students' families came to live in the United States. The teacher put the information on the table below. Use the information from the table to answer the questions about it.

Class Survey

Antarctica	Europe	Asia	North America	South America	Africa	Australia
0	7	4	3	4	6	1

1. Which continent did the most families come from to live in the U.S.?

   Antarctica   Africa   Europe
   ◯   ◯   ◯

2. Which continent did the fewest families come from to live in the U.S.?

   Antarctica   Asia   Australia
   ◯   ◯   ◯

3. Which continent did six families come from to live in the U.S.?

   North America   South America   Africa
   ◯   ◯   ◯

4. List the two continents that had the same number of families come to live in the U.S.

   1. _____

   2. _____

Directions: The school is celebrating International Week by serving food from a different country each day. Answer the questions below to show what foods were served to celebrate certain countries. Use a completely filled circle to mark your answer choice.

1. On Monday, China was celebrated with

   tacos.   rice.   bratwurst.
    ○   ○   ○

2. On Tuesday, Mexico was celebrated with

   spaghetti.   tacos.   rice.
    ○   ○   ○

3. On Wednesday, Italy was celebrated with

   tacos.   spaghetti.   bratwurst.
    ○   ○   ○

4. On Thursday, Germany was celebrated with

   bratwurst.   rice.   hot dogs.
    ○   ○   ○

5. On Friday, the United States was celebrated with

   hot dogs.   rice.   tacos.
    ○   ○   ○

Contributions of Different Cultures Within the U.S.

Directions: Answer the four questions using the map, the compass, and the map key. Use a completely filled circle to mark your answer choice.

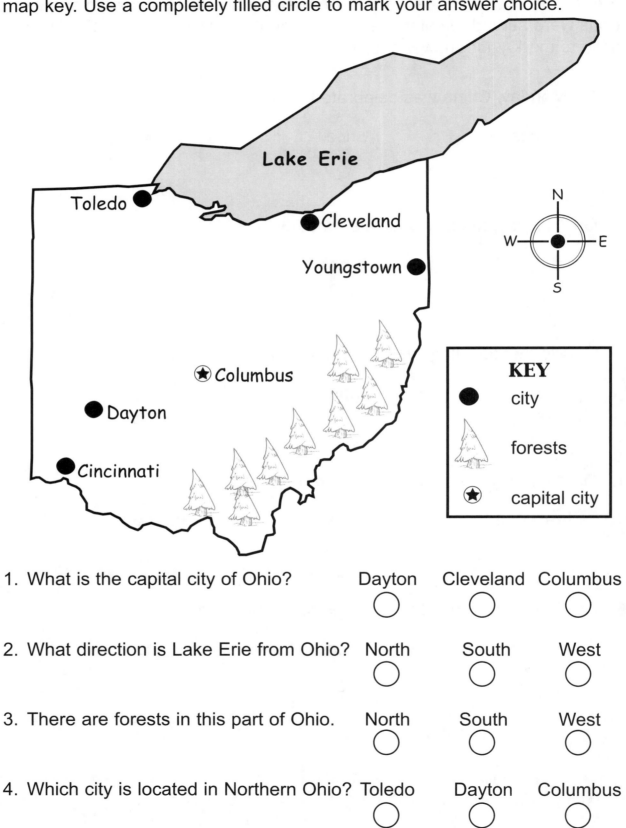

1. What is the capital city of Ohio?   Dayton   Cleveland   Columbus
                                            ◯   ◯   ◯

2. What direction is Lake Erie from Ohio?   North   South   West
                                            ◯   ◯   ◯

3. There are forests in this part of Ohio. North   South   West
                                            ◯   ◯   ◯

4. Which city is located in Northern Ohio? Toledo   Dayton   Columbus
                                            ◯   ◯   ◯

Directions: Use the world map and compass to answer the questions below.

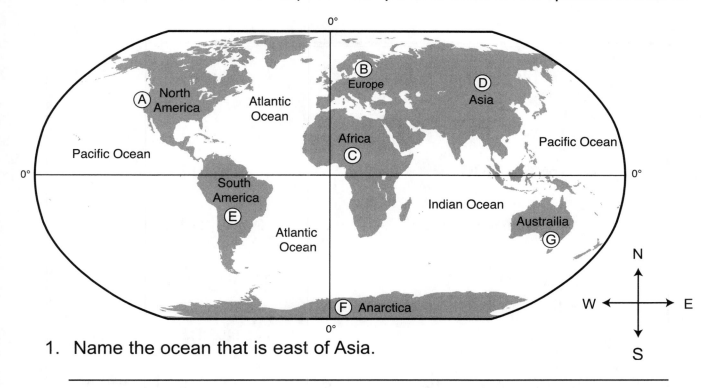

1. Name the ocean that is east of Asia.

   _____

   _

   _____

2. Name the continent at point E.

   _____

   _

   _____

3. What ocean is west of North America?

   _____

   _

   _____

4. Name the continent at point B.

   _____

   _

   _____

Directions: Use the chart below to fill in the Venn diagram on the next page.

Urban	Rural
skyscrapers	roads
homes	cornfields
state offices	working people
roads	barns
working people	cows, pigs, and horses
shopping centers	homes

Directions: Use the words on the chart from page 106 to compare urban and rural communities on the Venn diagram.

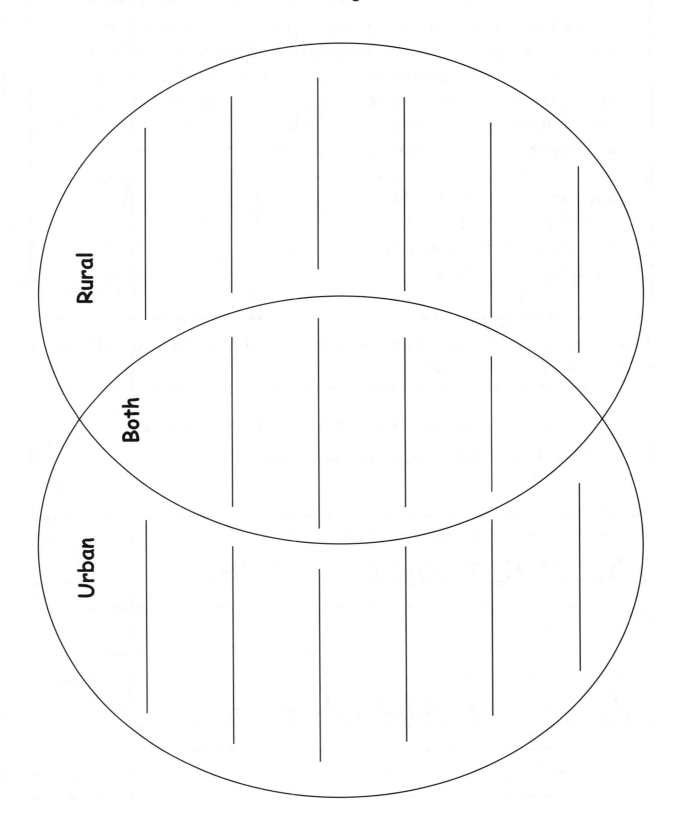

Directions: Read the selection below.

Lydia gave a report to the class about buyers and sellers. She decided to use her grandmother as an example. Lydia told the class that her grandmother is a seamstress. That means she makes clothes for people to buy. Lydia explained that her grandmother is a buyer because she has to buy all of the supplies she needs to make coats and pants and dresses, like fabric and buttons and thread.

She also explained that her grandmother is a seller when someone pays her money for the things she makes.

dress maker

dress buyer

Directions: Read the sentence about Marco. Then, explain how Marco is a buyer and a seller.

Marco is planning to sell lemonade at the school fair.

(Hint: Use Lydia's report above to help you.)

Marco is a buyer when he _____

_____

Marco is a seller when he _____

_____

Directions: Look at the picture below to help you answer the questions about it on the next page.

Rico, Anthony, and William went to a football game. The boys paid $2.00 each to get into the game. Rico told William and Anthony that in Mexico, it would cost 20 pesos to go to this football game. William said that in England, it would cost 1 British pound.

The boys used the chart below to find out how much the items at the concession stand would cost in U.S. dollars, in Mexican pesos, and in British pounds.

2 U.S. dollars	=	20 Mexican pesos	=	1 British pound
1 U.S. dollar	=	10 Mexican pesos	=	0.5 British pound

Directions: Use the charts on page 109 to answer the questions below. Write your answer on the line or use a completely filled circle to mark your answer choice.

1. William bought a hot dog for $1.00. How much does the hot dog cost in pesos?

    _____

    _____

2. Rico bought two slices of pizza. How many British pounds would he need?

    _____

    _____

3. How many pesos does Anthony need to buy a candy bar?

    5   10   20
    ○   ○   ○

4. William has 1 British pound. He can buy

    3 slices of pizza.   3 hot dogs.   1 slice of pizza & 1 hot dog.
    ○   ○   ○

5. Which of the forms of money has the most value?

    U.S. dollar   Mexican peso   British pound
    ○   ○   ○

Directions: Read the following information and use it to answer the questions below. Use a completely filled circle to mark your answer choice.

Miss Burns is talking to the class about the leaders who govern towns, cities, states, and the United States. She told the class that these leaders are elected by the people. People all over the United States can vote for the president. Only people living in Ohio can vote for the governor of Ohio. Only people living in a city or town can vote for that town's mayor.

1. Only people living in Ohio can vote for me.

   Governor of Ohio   President of the U.S.   City Mayor
        ◯   ◯   ◯

2. Only people living in my city can vote for me.

   Governor of Ohio   President of the U.S.   City Mayor
        ◯   ◯   ◯

3. Citizens of the United States can vote for me.

   Governor of Ohio   President of the U.S.   City Mayor
        ◯   ◯   ◯

Identify Leaders and How They Are Elected

Directions: Read the Computer Lab Rules in the illustration below. Use the rules to answer the questions that follow.

Computer Lab Rules

1. Be patient! Wait your turn to use the computer.
2. Stack the books on the table when you finish.
3. Computers are for classroom projects only.
4. Always be respectful of others.

1. Why is Rule #1 an important computer lab rule?

_____

_____

_____

_____

_____

2. What could happen if someone broke Rule #4?

_____

_____

_____

_____

Directions: Read each sentence below and decide what citizenship trait the person in the sentence is displaying. Use a completely filled circle to mark your answer choice.

1. Mr. Sadler stood up when the American flag passed by during the parade.

    honesty   persistence   patriotism
       ○   ○   ○

2. Amy returned the extra candy bar that was put in her bag by mistake.

    confidence   honesty   persistence
       ○   ○   ○

3. Martin kept asking the mayor to buy new equipment for the park.

    persistence   patriotism   honesty
       ○   ○   ○

4. Becky knew she was well-prepared for the class presentation.

    patriotism   self-assurance   respect others
       ○   ○   ○

Demonstrate Citizenship Traits   113

Directions: You are preparing a school report. Answer the questions below about what sources you would use to find information for your report. Use a completely filled circle to mark your answer choice.

Which resource would you use to:

1. gather information about Ohio's history from 1900-2000?

   ◯ a dictionary
   ◯ a map of the United States
   ◯ a book titled *Ohio History*

2. list the last ten presidents of the United States?

   ◯ a computer search
   ◯ a book titled *Ohio History*
   ◯ a globe

3. find the countries that are located on the equator?

   ○ a map of the United States
   ○ a globe
   ○ a book titled *Ohio History*

4. find definitions for the mayor, governor, and president?

   ○ a dictionary
   ○ an atlas
   ○ a map of the United States

5. find the distance from the school to the state capital of Ohio?

   ○ a map of South America
   ○ an atlas
   ○ an encyclopedia

6. find out about your family's history?

   ○ a family relative
   ○ a map of the United States
   ○ a book titled *Ohio History*

7. find out about crops grown in Ohio?

   ○ a map of the United States
   ○ an almanac
   ○ a globe

Directions: Cut out the pictures on the next page. Glue the pictures in the boxes below to show the correct order from resource to product.

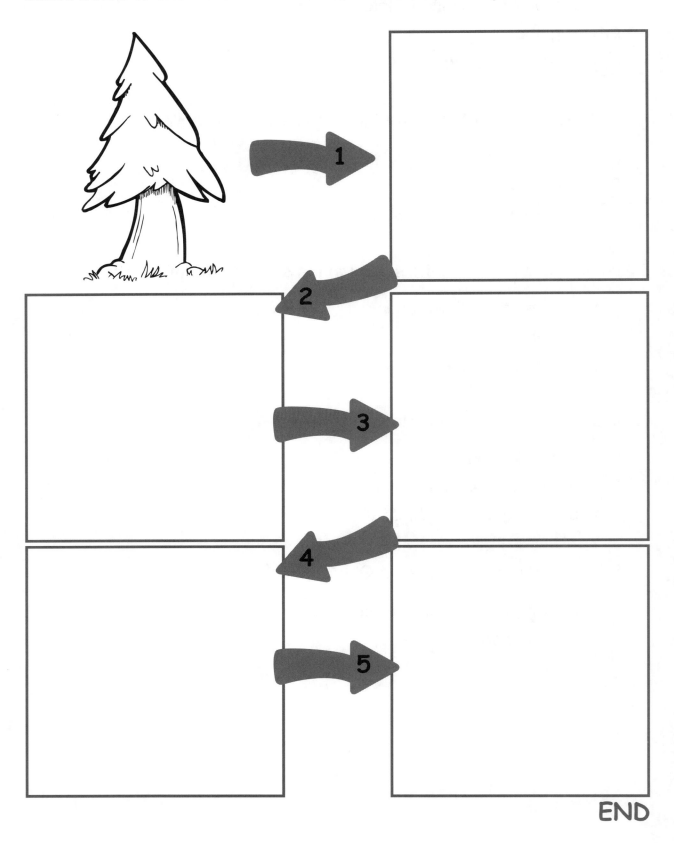

END

Events in a Sequence (1 of 2)

Directions: Cut out the pictures below along the dotted lines. Use them to complete the activity on page 116.

Science

The Science chapter of this workbook will help you practice answering many questions using different types of information. You will use a completely filled circle for multiple-choice, write a word, a phrase, or a complete sentence for a short-answer, and write two or more sentences with extra details for an extended-response.

You will be asked to read charts, tables, graphs, and simple keys, then use that information to answer questions. Use all the skills you have learned about collecting, interpreting, and evaluating scientific information to help you understand what you are being asked.

Use this Science Checklist to remind you to complete each workbook page carefully.

✔ Science Checklist

- ☐ I read or listened to the information carefully.

- ☐ I used the illustrations, graphs, or tables to help me understand the information better.

- ☐ I followed the directions that were given.

- ☐ I used the correct response on the page—a completely filled circle, a short answer, or an extended response.

- ☐ I answered all the questions on the page.

- ☐ I checked my answers carefully.

Directions: Look at the pictures below. Use the information on each picture to help you answer the questions. Use a completely filled circle to mark your answer choice.

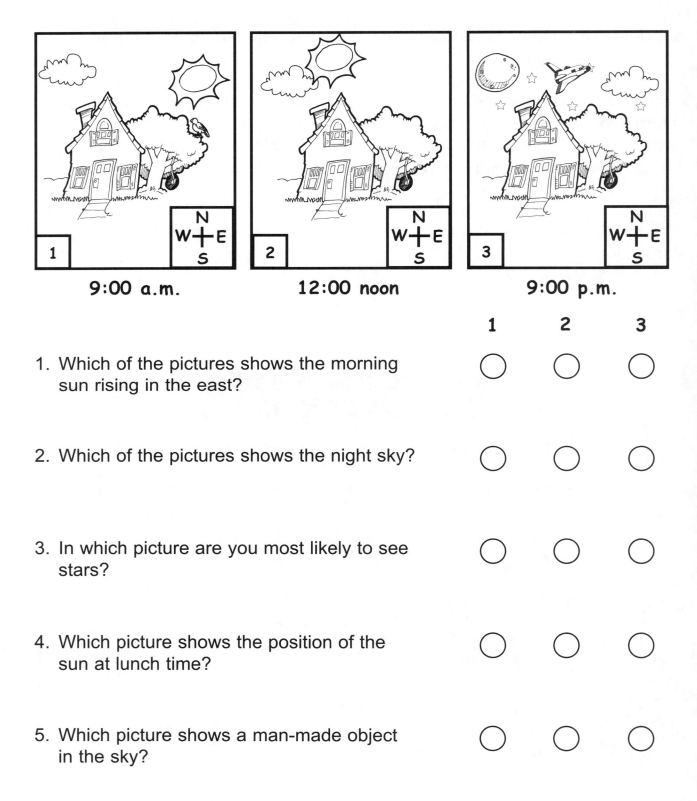

		1	2	3
1.	Which of the pictures shows the morning sun rising in the east?	◯	◯	◯
2.	Which of the pictures shows the night sky?	◯	◯	◯
3.	In which picture are you most likely to see stars?	◯	◯	◯
4.	Which picture shows the position of the sun at lunch time?	◯	◯	◯
5.	Which picture shows a man-made object in the sky?	◯	◯	◯

Directions: Use what you know about the movement of the sun to draw where the sun will be at 6:30 p.m.

6:30 p.m.

Explain your drawing of the sun's position.

_____

—————————————————————————————————————

═════════════════════════════════════

—————————————————————————————————————

═════════════════════════════════════

—————————————————————————————————————

═════════════════════════════════════

—————————————————————————————————————

═════════════════════════════════════

—————————————————————————————————————

Directions: The second graders at Central Elementary School created a calendar to show the phases of the moon during March. Use the data illustrated on their calendar to answer the questions below.

Phases of the Moon					
	New Moon	First Quarter Moon	Full Moon	Last Quarter Moon	

March

Sunday	Monday	Tuesday	Wednesday	Thursday	Friday	Saturday
			1 🌑	2	3	4
5	6	7	8	9 🌓	10	11
12	13	14	15	16 🌕	17	18
19	20 First Day of Spring	21	22	23 🌗	24	25
26	27	28	29	30 🌑	31	

1. How many new moons occurred during the month? _____

2. On which day of the week was there a full moon? _____

3. How many phases are there in the moon cycle? _____

4. The moon changes slowly from one phase to the next. Draw what you think the moon might look like as it changes from a full moon to a quarter moon.

Full Moon

Last Quarter Moon

Directions: Look at pictures A and B. Draw a picture of how the tree will look in the next season.

1.

A	B	Next Season

2.

A	B	Next Season

3.

A	B	Next Season

4. Describe your favorite season of the year.

_____

_____

_____

_____

_____

Weather Changes/Repeating Seasonal Pattern   123

Directions: Read each phrase below and choose which season it describes. Use a completely filled circle to mark your answer choice.

1. a hot, humid day at an amusement park

   ◯ winter   ◯ summer   ◯ fall

2. a blizzard that closes school for a snow day

   ◯ winter   ◯ summer   ◯ spring

3. warming temperatures causing Lake Erie to thaw

   ◯ summer   ◯ fall   ◯ spring

4. cooling temperatures and brisk winds

   ◯ summer   ◯ winter   ◯ fall

5. a temperature of 94° F

   ◯ winter   ◯ spring   ◯ summer

6. a temperature below 0° F

   ◯ summer   ◯ fall   ◯ winter

Directions: Fill in one or both circles to complete the dichotomous key. Which living thing does the key describe? Is it a frog or a dandelion?

frog   dandelion

Am I a   or a   ?

	frog	dandelion
1. I need air to survive.	○	○
2. I need water to survive.	○	○
3. I need living space.	○	○
4. I use sunlight to make food.	○	○

5. The living thing described is a _____.

6. Explain how you decided which living thing was described.

_____

_____

_____

_____

_____

_____

Directions: List five living things that can survive in a pond.

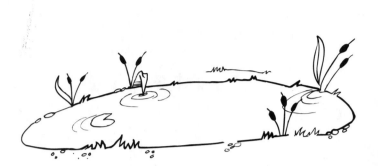

1. _____

2. _____

3. _____

4. _____

5. _____

List five living things that can survive in a forest.

1. _____

2. _____

3. _____

4. _____

5. _____

Name one living thing that might live in both of these environments.

_____

_____

_____

Directions: Look at the living thing pictured, then choose something it must have to live. Use a completely filled circle to mark your answer choice.

1.
○ milk
○ water
○ juice

2.
○ bird cage
○ food
○ birdbath

3.
○ hair bow
○ boots
○ food

4.
○ flower pot
○ garden
○ sunlight

5.
○ food
○ toys
○ candy

6.
○ saddle
○ horseshoe
○ hay

7.
○ river
○ grass
○ glasses

8.
○ collar
○ leash
○ water

Directions: Look at the two trees pictured and fill in one or both circles in the simple key. Then, answer the two questions that follow. Use a completely filled circle to mark your answer choice.

evergreen tree   **maple tree**

1. This tree has a trunk.   ◯   ◯

2. This tree has bark.   ◯   ◯

3. This tree is found in Ohio.   ◯   ◯

4. This tree changes color in autumn.   ◯   ◯

5. Which tree is best described by this key?

   _____

6. List some words to describe this tree.

   _____

   _____

   _____

   _____

   _____

   _____

   _____

Directions: Choose a word from the word bank to answer each of the following riddles.

Word Bank			
gills	leaves	roots	lungs
webbed feet	wings	fur	bark

1. I help fish live underwater. What am I?

2. I help plants get nutrients from the soil. What am I?

3. I help a plant gather light to make food. What am I?

4. I help a duck move swiftly through the water. What am I?

5. I help birds fly. What am I?

6. I help humans breathe. What am I?

7. I am the covering that keeps animals warm in winter. What am I?

Directions: Draw a line from the organism in the left column to the way it prepares for a seasonal change described in the right column.

1.

    moves deeper underground

2.

    wears warmer clothing

3.

    buries nuts

4.

    increases coat fur

5.

    moves deeper underwater

6.

    migrates south

7. Tell how deciduous (leaf bearing) trees in Ohio prepare for the winter.

_____

_____

_____

_____

Directions: Cut out the stages in the life cycle of a pumpkin below. Use them to complete the activity on page 133 of a pumpkin.

Compare Ohio Plants During Seasons (1 of 2)

Directions: Cut out the pictures that show the stages in the life cycle of a pumpkin on page 131. Glue them on the diagram below to show the life cycle of a pumpkin.

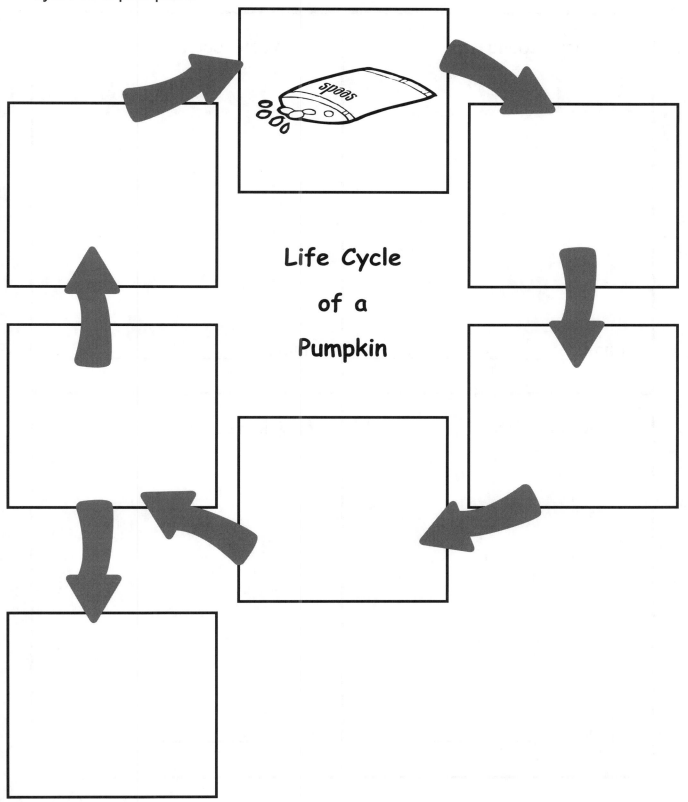

Life Cycle

of a

Pumpkin

Directions: Draw and name an object that makes the sound listed in each of the boxes below.

1. A loud sound	2. A soft sound
name _____	name _____
3. A high sound	4. A low sound
name _____	name _____

Directions: For show and tell, Chip wanted to show the class how to make shadows on the wall. He turned off the lights in the classroom and then turned on his flashlight. The students could see the beam of light traveling in a straight line coming from Chip's flashlight.

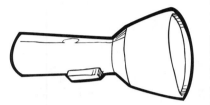  

He made shadows using several objects and asked students to try and guess each object. The shadows looked like the ones below. Write the name of the object that made each shadow on the line.

Shadow   **Object that made shadow**

1. _____

2. _____

3. _____

4. _____

5. _____

6. _____

Directions: Miss Lennon gave each group of students in her class a box of objects to use in constructing a new object. The contents of group 1's box are pictured below. Look at the items.

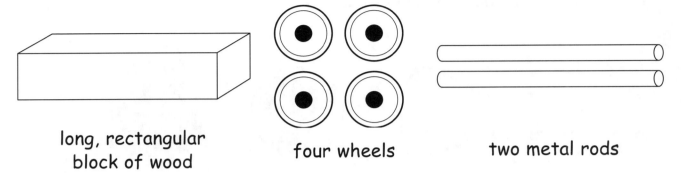

long, rectangular
block of wood

four wheels

two metal rods

Design an object with some or all of the items. Draw a picture of your completed object and tell how you would use it or how it works.

Drawing

Explanation

Directions: Read the rules written in the boxes below. Use a completely filled circle to show those rules that make the science lab a safe place for students.

◯   1. Handle scientific tools with care.

◯   2. Running is permitted on the playground.

◯   3. Always have an adult present.

◯   4. Always watch and do what other students do.

◯   5. Wash your hands after doing science experiments.

◯   6. Always wash your hands after handling seeds and leaves.

Directions: Look at the table showing scientific instruments. Read each phrase, the select the correct tool for each purpose. Write the name of the science tool on the line.

1. checking the outside temperature _____

2. measuring the length of your foot _____

3. closely examining details of an organism _____

4. measuring four quarts of water _____

5. comparing the weights of two objects at the same time _____

6. recording the time it takes for a seed to sprout _____

7. determining how much you weigh _____

8. setting the correct time on the hour _____

Scientific Instruments

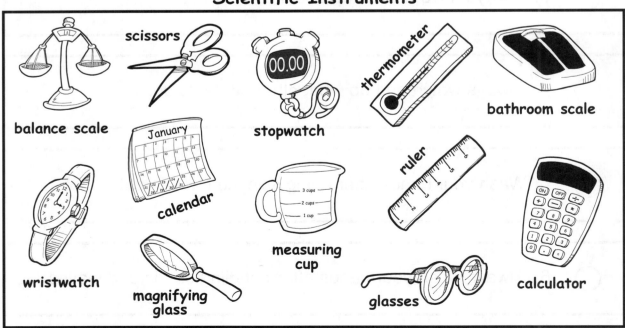

balance scale scissors stopwatch thermometer bathroom scale January calendar wristwatch measuring cup ruler calculator magnifying glass glasses

Directions: Use a completely filled circle to show the correct measurement in U.S. Standard or metric units.

1.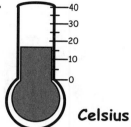

Celsius

○ 16° Celsius

○ 20° Celsius

○ 20° Fahrenheit

2.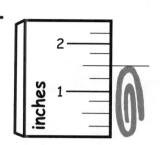

○ $1\frac{1}{2}$ centimeters

○ 1 inch

○ $1\frac{1}{2}$ inches

3.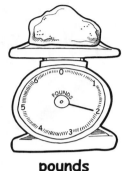

pounds

○ 2 ounces

○ 2 kilograms

○ 2 pounds

4.

○ 2 centimeters

○ 3 inches

○ 2 inches

5.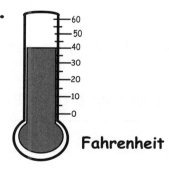

Fahrenheit

○ 40° Celsius

○ 50° Fahrenheit

○ 40° Fahrenheit

6.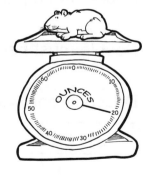

ounces

○ 20 pounds

○ 20 ounces

○ 20 grams

Directions: Follow the arrows on the diagram to see what happened to the trees. Use a completely filled circle to mark your answer choice.

	Yes	No
1. The trees were cut down to build houses.	◯	◯
2. The forest is a home for living things.	◯	◯
3. Some living things lose their homes when trees are cut down.	◯	◯
4. People need places to live.	◯	◯
5. People must help to keep the environment safe.	◯	◯

6. Describe one way you can help protect the environment.

_____

_____

_____

_____

_____

_____

Solution to a Problem Might Affect People/Environment

Notes

Notes

Congratulations

To: _____

You have successfully completed

**Ready, Set,
Show What
You Know®**

2nd Grade

Parent/Teacher: _____

Date: _____

Thank YOU
For Your Purchase!

Show What You Know® Publishing is dedicated to developing quality educational products and services for you and your students. We are committed to creating supplemental materials for grades K–12, specializing in standards-based test preparation.

Other preparation materials include books and flash cards.

Call 1-877-PASSING (727-7464) for a *FREE* catalog or visit our website: www.showwhatyouknowpublishing.com